P9-CFL-215

Smart

Is the New

Rich

Smart
Is the New
Rich

Money Guide for Millennials

CHRISTINE ROMANS

WILEY

Copyright © 2015 by Christine Romans. All rights reserved.

Published by John Wiley & Sons, Inc., Hoboken, New Jersey.
Published simultaneously in Canada.

For general information on our other products and services or for technical support, please contact our Customer Care Department within the United States at (800) 762-2974, outside the United States at (317) 572-3993 or fax (317) 572-4002.

Wiley publishes in a variety of print and electronic formats and by print-on-demand. Some material included with standard print versions of this book may not be included in e-books or in print-on-demand. If this book refers to media such as a CD or DVD that is not included in the version you purchased, you may download this material at http://booksupport.wiley.com. For more information about Wiley products, visit www.wiley.com.

Library of Congress Cataloging-in-Publication Data is on file.

ISBN 9781118949351 (Hardcover)
ISBN 9781118949375 (ePDF)
ISBN 9781118949368 (ePub)

Printed in the United States of America
10 9 8 7 6 5 4 3 2 1

*To my parents
for teaching me the value of the dollar,
and that happiness isn't about money.*

Contents

Preface

I remember the exact moment the power, influence, and potential of your generation first struck me.

It was midnight, four hours after the first polls closed in the 2012 presidential election. My colleague John King handed off CNN's "magic wall" to me and I quickly began studying the exit polling data. Surrounded by swooping cameras and a blinding grid of lighting, I stood in the CNN Election Center tapping through and cross-referencing table after table of numbers and responses from voters who had just left the voting booth.

Barack Obama had been reelected president of the United States just hours before, and the numbers were rolling in throughout the night telling us who voted and why. Measures for same-sex marriage were on the ballot and passed in three states. Washington and Colorado legalized marijuana. In all, there were 180 ballot measures in 38 states. As I scrolled through the results, I was struck by the fact that your generation had become a power player in social change in the United States. Those polls showed a generation that considers itself innovative and diverse. One that is open-minded and, better yet, flexible enough to *change* your mind. You have values you believe in, but you respect others' values. As I clicked, tapped, and dragged data across that magic wall, it became quite clear that this generation known as *millennials* is one to be reckoned with.

And you are different from your elders.

All of my reporting shows you are the first generation to value experience over possessions, which is a huge change for a U.S. economy based on the idea of me, more, now. Your parents' generation bought bigger houses, cars, boats, and second homes, and they spent more time planning vacations than their retirement—all thanks to a mirage of easy credit. But that's over—and you know it.

You're a generation forged by the Great Recession, the War on Terror, and an explosion of consumer technology no generation before you could have dreamed of. You've grown up comfortable with technology, and you expect it to change the world. And that technology brings you different experiences and values that you put above most other "things." Look no further than the ideological and economic heart of this country right now, thriving with millennials at the helm: Silicon Valley. Understated is better. T-shirts, jeans, and ideas trump Wall Street bling, pinstripes, and financial engineering. Yahoo! CEO Marissa Mayer's car of choice sums it up: She drives a BMW that's nearly 20 years old!

You are the most educated generation in American history, and you have the student loan debt to show for it. But you are also coming into your prime spending years, which makes you the most coveted consumers in the world—tech-savvy, discriminating, and young. Companies spend more money marketing to you than to anyone else. Your brand loyalty is the holy grail; you've got 40-plus years of spending ahead of you, and everyone wants your money.

I want you to spend your money in ways that make you happy, but I also want to help you begin to save some and grow it.

Why write a money book for millennials? Because you have the most valuable ingredient for building wealth: time.

Money can't buy time. You have it for free.

It is the single most valuable ingredient in building wealth. And since you already picked up this book, you clearly have the will to put it to work.

Here's what these pages hold for you.

I've written this book to be read start to finish for a comprehensive look at managing your money: From your student loans to credit cards to investing for the first time. Or you can choose the chapters that speak most to your situation: negotiating your first job (Chapter 7) or building your credit score (Chapter 9). As the book title suggests, *this is a guide*. Just as the guidebook you would buy before a backpacking trip through Denmark or a honeymoon in Brazil, this guidebook combines my years of reporting on your generation and money with tips and tools to help you start building your wealth.

At the end of each chapter is an Action Plan—essentially the things you can do *today* to build wealth.

Chapter 1 gives you the budgeting basics that will help you build the mentality to save and the tools to get you started.

Chapter 2 shows how to choose a major, and how to make any major work in the postcollege rat race.

Chapter 3 reveals the smart ways to pay down student debt and still build for the future.

Chapter 4 is the essential read on the state of the U.S. labor market and your place in it. Anyone looking for a job and trying to excel in that job needs to know what's happening in the most dynamic labor market on earth. This is a critical macroeconomic look at the place that will be the engine of your personal economy—the job market.

Chapter 5 is the millennial handbook for getting ahead at work: how to interview for and negotiate your first salary. Does the thought of a nine-to-five job at an office of gen x-ers and baby boomers terrify you? How do you start your own company and make work work for you? Should you "lean in" or "lean back" at work? We will explore the subtle gender differences in the workplace, with advice about the different ways men and women negotiate. Remember, the salary you accept at the beginning is the starting line for a 40-year career. Where you start is critical.

Will you buy or rent? Chapter 6 offers strategies for the biggest questions in real estate, including how to survive living at home with your parents, how to split the rent bill with your roommate, and how to get your roommate's ubiquitous boy/girlfriend to kick in some of the rent, too.

Couples and families are more likely to talk about religion, politics, or sex than money. Chapter 7 explores how to frankly talk with your parents about money (and borrow some from them). And it discusses the right questions to ask early in a relationship to make sure you are a good money match. Is it appropriate to ask how much the other person owes in student loans on the third date?

Some of you may want to skip ahead to the investing chapter—of all the money moves you make, investing early will have the biggest impact on where you end up. Most of your grandparents could rely on a pension for their retirement, and your parents lean on a 401(k) for life after work. But you millennials will have even fewer investment tools handed to you when it comes to securing your financial health and wealth. So it's up to you.

Consider this: If you save $5,000 a year for five years in your twenties and then never invest a dime again, you'll have more money in your retirement than someone saving $5,000 a year all through their thirties and beyond. Chapter 8 shows you the common traits of 401(k) millionaires. (Hint: Time is on your side again.)

There's good debt—mostly student loans and mortgages—and bad debt—almost always credit cards. Chapter 9 offers valuable help for keeping your debts in perspective, with tricks for paying down the good debt and obliterating the bad debt, and how that will affect your credit score. The credit score is your money IQ. We look at how to keep it high and what to do to fix it if it is low.

My hope is that, whether you read this book straight through or choose the chapters that mean the most to your own personal finances, you'll find advice and information in these pages that will empower you to start planning your financial future now.

Christine Romans
September 2014

Acknowledgments

This book would not be possible without the considerable efforts of my husband, Ed Tobin, whose encouragement made me think I could actually write a third book while raising three young boys and working a full-time job, and whose news judgment and editing made it actually happen.

I'm so fortunate to be surrounded by the phenomenal reporters and editors at *CNNMoney*, who peel back the economic statistics and show how they matter to our readers and viewers. For any of you settling down with this book, make no mistake, CNNMoney.com will be a valuable resource as you use the building blocks within these pages to grow your wealth.

Special thanks to certified financial planners Ryan Mack from Optimum Capital Management and Doug Flynn from Flynn Zito, who entertained my endless questions about retirement planning, budgets, and investing. To Mitch Tuchman of Rebalance IRA for tailoring an investing plan precisely for *Smart Is the New Rich* readers and to Stephanie Genkin for sharing in these pages the aspirations of her millennial clients.

To the many millennials we interviewed for this book, and whose anecdotes are within these pages: Thanks for your honesty and, no, I didn't use your last names!

A special thanks to my producer, the brilliant Logan Whiteside, who loves numbers as much as I do and scours the monthly labor market reports with me with equal glee. To my coanchor, John Berman, who makes a 3:00 a.m. wake-up (almost) fun. To CNN president Jeff Zucker, thank you for making Berman and me wake up before 3:00 a.m.! But more importantly, thank you for the encouragement to follow my passion for education and economics coverage.

To CNNMoney's Laurie Frankel and Mike Tarson, thank you for your wonky love of tax-deferred versus taxable retirement strategies and dogged reporting on education and real estate, respectively!

Special thank-you to the folks at Wiley and NS Bienstock for your support.

CHAPTER 1

How to Think About Money: Budgeting Basics

> I think the best advice I've ever received is to plan for the future and to save your money. To plan for the future in a way you can have the same lifestyle after you've finished your job? That takes some planning and saving.
>
> —Danica Patrick[1]

The common denominator of so many successful people I interview is an urge to save money and build for the future. Danica Patrick is the most successful woman in U.S. auto racing—a race car driver, fashion model, and marketing maven. The best advice she ever received? How to take the last turn, how to navigate the pit, how to get the most out of the last drop of fuel? No, the best advice she ever received—and gives to others—is simple and classic. Save your money.

It's really not complicated at all. Money saved today and invested properly—amplified by time—means wealth in the future. It's the little black dress of prosperity. It never goes out of style. Among the many gems from legendary investor Warren Buffett, this sums it up best: "Someone is sitting in the shade today because someone planted a tree a long time ago."[2]

No one is going to plant that tree for you. The key words here are *you* and *time*. Unless you win the lottery (you won't) or have a trust fund (nice, but unlikely) or have the brain of Mark Zuckerberg (don't we all wish?), you will grow wealth only one way: by spending less money than you earn. Investing *your* savings over time grows wealth.

> ## PROSPERITY FORMULA
>
> Earnings − Spending = Savings
>
> Savings × Time = Wealth

There is a surefire, can't-miss way for millennials, loosely defined as young adults ages 18 to 35, to become millionaires. Call it a get-rich-not-so-quick scheme. Fidelity Investments studied the habits of people who earned less than $150,000 a year but had retirement account balances topping $1,000,000.[3]

What's the secret of these 401(k) millionaires? They started saving young, and they socked away a big part of their paychecks. How big? Fourteen percent of their pay each year—before any company match in a 401(k).

They started young, maxed out their savings, and took the "free money" that is the 401(k) company match—that is, the money your employer offers to contribute to your 401(k) plan. They weren't too conservative in their portfolios. The younger you are, the more stocks you should own. In fact, on average they had 70 percent of their retirement savings in stocks. (Bonds and savings accounts yield very low returns for savers and conservative investors. More on this, and alternative investments if your employer does *not* offer a 401(k), in Chapter 8.)

Bottom line: They started early. And you can, too.

Let's make something clear from the start if we are to spend the upcoming pages together. I don't believe you are a generation of lazy, narcissistic, reckless-spending, entitled tech junkies. (A Google search of the term "millennial" or "gen y" is entertaining.) In fact, I'm incredibly optimistic about the innovation and open-mindedness you're already bringing with you to the workplace. As I have crossed the country speaking with students and graduates and reporting on companies and economics, I have found that, despite the pile of bad luck you were dealt by the financial crisis, you are a generally optimistic and entrepreneurial bunch. You're the most educated generation in U.S. history, and you understand technology in an intuitive way that no other generation can.

The economy is slowly healing, and you're poised to succeed. I'm more optimistic by the day about your job prospects. Hiring for the class of 2014 jumped a stunning 8.6 percent from 2013.[4] Whether they're looking for accounting, computer science, engineering, or M.B.A. graduates, more than half of companies surveyed reported they were stepping up their hiring.

We'll discuss the job landscape further in Chapter 4, but for the purposes of how you *think* about money, the subject of this chapter comes against an improving backdrop. The jobs market is healing. The current recovery was among the slowest postrecession jobs recoveries, but finally all the millions of jobs lost in the Great Recession have been recovered.[5] Technology will provide new opportunities we can't even predict today. And your generation—innovative by nature—will play a central role in that.

Yes, there is a considerable problem of too much student debt and too few jobs for recent graduates. But I don't think that all millennials have been permanently sidelined by their student loans, nor have they been permanently left out of the jobs market. We'll explore managing that debt in Chapter 2 and getting a job in Chapter 5, but in this discussion of how you think about money, it's time to relegate debt and jobs to background noise. Repeat after me: You have something to offer the workforce, and you can manage your student loans.

The typical student loan burden can be manageable. According to a report from the Brookings Institution, just 7 percent of households with student debt have a burden of $50,000 or higher.[6] About a third of bachelor's degree graduates have no debt at all, and the average debt of those who do hovers around $30,000. There is a rule of thumb in college savings and planning: You can afford to borrow for college about as much as you expect to earn in your first year's salary. If you are the typical business major, that means you can afford to borrow around $50,000. Humanities and social science graduates can afford to borrow less.[7] The average starting salary for the class of 2014 rose 1.2 percent from the prior year, to $45,473, according to the National Association of Colleges and Employers (NACE),[8] with wide variations by discipline (Table 1.1).

If your student loans are getting you down, remember this: A college graduate will earn, on average, a million dollars more over the course of a working career than a high school grad.[9] Handling student debt diligently

Table 1.1   Average Salaries by Discipline

Business	$53,901
Communications	$43,924
Computer Science	$61,741
Education	$40,863
Engineering	$62,719
Health Sciences	$51,541
Humanities and Social Sciences	$38,365
Math and Sciences	$43,414

Source: National Association of Colleges and Employers

will be a key part in your strategy for building wealth. The vast majority of college borrowers with less than $50,000 in student loan debt can certainly be moving forward in their financial lives and using their best asset—time—to work for them. Don't let anyone tell you it's impossible to plan for the future while still paying off the past. It can be done. (Chapter 3 will help you organize your approach to managing debt.)

This is not a book for defeatists. It's a book for young people of any means who want to build wealth. Whether you have loan debt, were fortunate enough to graduate debt-free, or are considering college or studying now, it is critical to save early and train yourself in habits to make your money grow.

Most of us didn't grow up reading the *Wall Street Journal,* and many high schools teach rudimentary economics if anything at all. In grade school, children still learn to count change, yet there is little if any real preparation for the dizzying array of college financing schemes, prepaid debit cards, peer-to-peer loans, and countless other accounts millennials get pitched every day. Financial literacy is not something the United States does well, and most families would rather talk about religion or politics than money. There's no shame in getting started now. The old cliche that it is better late than never does not apply here. You are reading these words now, and you have the most valuable ingredient you need: time.

In the workforce and in the headlines you have undoubtedly heard and read those old clichés attached to the newest generation. They don't work as hard. Consumer technology makes them lazy and entitled. They are selfish. However, a seminal study of millennials by the Wall Street research firm UBS found something very different—and very exciting—for any member of this generation looking for success. That study found that millennials have learned the lessons from the financial crises during which they grew up and are now primed to save more money and build wisely for the future. Think of your generation as being as powerful as the baby boomer generation—you will have an equally huge impact on the economy once you hit your stride financially.

> "Millennials shatter stereotypes, believe in hard work, worry about parents' financial health, and define success as a combination of money, healthy relationships, and enriching experiences."[10]
>
> —*UBS Investor Watch*

The UBS study found this generation more likely to save, more frugal, and more resilient than prior generations. UBS found that words like *entitled* and *lazy* don't fit the reality.

UBS ASKED MILLENNIALS TO DEFINE SUCCESS: HOW DO YOU KNOW WHEN YOU HAVE ARRIVED?

Emotional (39%)
- Having a happy family (45%).
- Having a deeply meaningful relationship with my spouse/partner (37%).
- Staying true to the values I believe in (18%).
- Leading a calm, simple life with people who care about me (17%).

Financial (30%)
- Having financial freedom (48%).
- Being able to provide for future generations of my family (15%).
- Being well-compensated for what I do (14%).
- Owning things I aspired to have, such as art, a second home, a boat, and so on (12%).

Experiential (24%)
- Living a full life with a wide variety of experiences (37%).
- Enjoying the work I do (29%).
- Being someone from whom others seek advice/opinions (4%).
- Knowing interesting, creative people (2%).

Achievement (7%)
- Achieving more than my parents or my peers (7%).
- Reaching a very senior job position, such as a C-Suite position (7%).
- Owning my own business (5%).
- Being able to give significantly to charity (3%).

Source: UBS

In fact, money matters to millennials, UBS found, but they fall short of the "greedy" tag one might apply to their elders. Success to millennials means hard work (69 percent), saving and living frugally (45 percent), and a good education (37 percent). And success is not just about money. This generation's definition of success is more nuanced, adding emotional and relationship factors to the formula and not just traditional measures of financial health.

Achieving that success takes some simple first steps. And the most critical is the monthly budget.

PAY YOURSELF FIRST

The first key to building wealth is to live below your means. The money you don't spend you put to work. For many years, it was the American way to spend more than we earned, using credit to pay for the rest. Millions of Americans burned through their money, justified by the false assumption that the price of their home would rise forever. Easy credit made people feel rich. When the recession hit, these spenders took the biggest hit financially. Today, *smart* is the new rich, and being smart begins with a budget. Even the word *budget* makes most of us cringe. It's a loaded word, full of limitations, that we think is more suitable for older generations. But a budget is the money version of a healthy diet. Once you identify the empty calories in your budget, you'll feel better and more focused.

A budget is simply a *plan*. And it's the nonnegotiable habit for growing wealth. Patrick O'Connell, executive vice president of the Ameriprise Advisor Group, works with thousands of financial advisers across the country. "The price of success is paid for in full in advance," he tells me. Having a budget and saving money every month is paying yourself first.

"We see many millennials interested in building wealth who have to start building the savings plan first. Pay yourself first, and work the expense base off the remainder," O'Connell says. He likes to start with these three steps:

Three Steps to Building Your Budget

1. Identify how you are spending money now.
2. Evaluate your current spending and then set goals that take into account your long-term financial objectives.
3. Trace your spending and make sure it stays within your guidelines.

Often, we feel as though we have a general idea of how much money is coming in and going out each month. But you've got to put down on paper every penny.

Financial expert Stephanie Genkin, a Brooklyn-based independent fee-only planner who advises millennials, says it's always possible to become a saver.

"I worked with a young woman who had no debt but liked to treat herself to expensive new clothes and books every month. We talked about what it would be like for her to scale back on her spending in order to put away a little money each month for retirement and a rainy-day fund. I got through to her by telling her what her life might be like 10 to 20 years from now without savings. She now contributes 3 percent to her 401(k) and automates a fixed amount of her paycheck to a savings account."

There are helpful online tools and budget apps like www.mint.com to analyze your habits and craft a budget. Check out your bank or credit union website for tools to use for budgeting, tracking your spending, and automatically paying bills. Websites for money managers Fidelity and Ameriprise Financial have helpful tips for organizing which bills to pay. It's incredibly important to really know how much you are spending each month in every single category. Only then can you spend less than you bring in and grow the difference.

I grew up with a frugal father, who had very simple rules about money that he often boiled down to entertaining little rhymes, one of which is the basis for every budget: "Keep your burn rate less than your earn rate." It means spend less than you earn. The budget helps you figure out how.

To get started, you need to ask yourself a few questions.

- Does your income money last as long as the month?
- Are you spending more than 28 percent of your take-home pay on housing costs?
- If you live at home, are you saving a little each month for a deposit on an apartment?
- Are you carrying a balance on your credit cards?
- If so, how many months will it take to be credit card debt–free?
- If your phone breaks, do you have money to get a new one?

- Your best friend from childhood just announced a destination wedding. Do you have the money to make it (not to mention the bachelor/bachelorette party)?
- If you have a job, does it offer a 401(k), and are you contributing enough to get the company match?
- Do you have three months' living expenses handy in case of an emergency?

Take note that I didn't even bother asking the age-old financial adviser question: At what age do you want to retire? That's because (1) it's nearly impossible for any young generation to really get their head around this question, since it's the last thing they think about; (2) forced savings plans like 401(k)s and IRAs (more on these in Chapter 8) help address the retirement issue; and (3) there are more pressing financial decisions facing millennials in the near term. Beyond the aforementioned "I have to pay for a new phone" dilemma, there are a host of other costs millennials have to prepare for, notes Ameriprise's O'Connell.

"Buying homes, selling homes, cars, children, weddings—you name it. So think about medium term financial goals and start building momentum. The first $5,000 or whatever your goal is to accumulate is the hardest," says O'Connell. "After you reach that first goal, it becomes easier. So you want to focus on a strong financial foundation."

HOW MUCH SHOULD YOU SAVE?

We'll more fully explore these questions, how to answer them, and how to get there in the pages ahead. Planning a budget means recognizing how far you are from these goals. You have to know what is coming in and going out before you can slot money for investments, real estate, and retirement goals. Write down every little expense—including the price of your morning bagel, change for doing laundry, the amounts for phone/Internet bills, and what you shell out for entertainment. Track your spending, make realistic goals, and be consistent. Once you're on track—with housing costs in line with what you can afford, high-interest credit card debt paid off, and student loan payments automatically paid each month—the next step is building wealth.

Throughout human history, civilizations endured because people planned for the future by socking away a little of today's wealth for the next year. They saved some of this year's crop to plant again the next year to guarantee stability (and wealth) for coming years. Eat all your seed corn now, and you'll starve later. It sounds rather *Game of Thrones*, I know, but, really, unless you budget, save, and prepare, you're leaving an awful lot to luck.

That's a bleak way of saying that Americans spend too much and save too little. On average, Americans save about 4 percent of their income each month. The savings rate has slowly improved since the Great Recession ended, but it still is not high enough. A reachable target is 10 percent, and those Fidelity 401(k) millionaires put away 14 percent on average, starting young.

As you prepare your budget, if you can't get to 10 percent right away, start more slowly. Squeeze just 1 percent out the first month, then 2 percent the next month. Ratchet up the savings, and trim the spending bit by bit.

"You've got to save every penny."

—*Carmelo Anthony, New York Knicks, CNN March 2012*

I often hear from readers and viewers that they don't have any money to save, that their finances are out of their control, and that until they get a better job or move to a different city or pay off their student loans, they can't save another penny.

I always circle back to the advice from my friend and frequent *CNNMoney* guest Ryan Mack. He's the president of Optimum Capital Management, and he is a true believer that anyone can make a budget and find money to save in it, no matter their circumstances. His mother raised two sons with scant money, sometimes on public assistance and in public housing. She made it into the middle class, and Mack uses her example in his own business to inspire anyone to build wealth. He says wealth is built slowly and surely through the little daily decisions we make with our money. He says all of us have a responsibility to be "good stewards" of our finances. Mack explains:

The good steward is my own mother who didn't have a lot of money to raise her two children but spent her days shopping at a thrift store, cutting coupons, and working her way off subsidized living in a way that allowed her to purchase her first home. The good steward understands that it is never about how much money you make, it is all about what you do with the money you make. It isn't about spending money to make an impression on others. It is all about spending money to make an impression on those personal goals and values that you find to be important to keep on your path to creating a financial legacy for future generations. This steward takes risks, lives within their means, but most importantly when they analyze their online spending statement, more often than not they purchased items that moved their household forward and didn't detract from its value.

Take a look at the online spending record of your credit card bill or check your bank statement for the past few months and try to divine the priorities that statement suggests about you. Is eating out more important than buying new clothes? Do you have an iTunes addiction? Is your Netflix bill off the charts? Love a daily latte? Without a budget, you have no idea how much you are spending each month on these things.

What you find may surprise you. In its report "Young America and Its Vices. Beer. McDonald's. Starbucks," Level Money (which offers a simple budgeting app for people 35 and under) found millennials spending big money in three major categories: coffee, burgers, and booze.[11] Turns out cash-strapped millennials still find plenty of money to spend on tastes-good-but-not-so-healthy options. Spending varies widely by region, but Level Money found the highest spending on booze in Massachusetts, Colorado, and New York and the highest spending on coffee solidly in the Northeast (Table 1.2).

Young people in the South spend more than twice what their New England cousins spend on fast food (Table 1.3). Top venues? McDon-

Table 1.2   Caffeine Addicts

State	Average annual spending	% purchasing more than once a week
Maine	$307	15%
Massachusetts	$277	12%
New Hampshire	$263	12%

Source: "Young America and Its Vices," Level Money

Table 1.3   Fast-Food Fanatics

	Average annual spending	% purchasing more than once a week
1. Oklahoma	$1,194	40%
2. Kansas	$1,040	35%
3. Texas	$978	35%
10. Colorado	$858	26%
48. New York	$485	11%
49. Connecticut	$471	10%
50. Vermont	$431	6%

Source: "Young America and Its Vices," Level Money

ald's, Chipotle, and Subway. This is proof that there is money in the budget for saving, even by squeezing just a little. For anyone looking to trim discretionary spending, these "vices" are the obvious first place to look.

The Level Money app automatically recommends a savings rate of 7 percent, but before you can get there you need to visualize how much you are spending. Apps and software can help with real-time organizing of expenses and income (beware, you will have to provide passwords for all your accounts so the budget apps can keep track), but often the best way to start is decidedly low-tech. Your grandparents put money into different envelopes labeled, for example, "Food," "Shelter," "Clothing," "Car," "Insurance," and "Extra." Simplistic? Yes. But it's a good way to start before you commit to one of the many digital budget tools available. (The suite of offerings is changing quickly. You can find a *New York Times* analysis of some of the veterans and a few more recent budgeting apps for millennials at this site: http://www.nytimes.com/2014/01/04/your-money/household-budgeting/review-apps-to-track-income-and-expenses.html?_r=0.)

Financial planner Ryan Mack says a good budget makes a good steward of saving.

"The good steward is the guy who was interviewed on CNN who never made over $13 per hour his entire life but was worth over $2 million after the age of 70," Mack says.

No matter how much money you make, you can build wealth. First come the smart daily decisions about spending money. Then comes saving what is left over.

THE RAINY-DAY FUND

No hidden meaning here—we all have to plan for the day when we lose our job or get hit with some other unexpected expense. So how much should you save?

Conservative financial planners recommend keeping six to nine months of your living expenses liquid. Others advise three to six months in normal times. (The term *liquid* means the funds are available for an emergency without too much trouble accessing them.) Either recommendation can sound daunting for people just getting control of their financial plans and not worthwhile for younger investors feeling invincible.

But it is critical that you work the rainy-day fund into your financial strategy.

So where can you stash it? Not in the mattress, of course, but putting it in the bank feels almost like the same thing. This is a terrible time for savings in this country because low interest rates mean you are not getting paid much for the bank to hold and use your money. The proliferation of bank fees and penalties means that, with just a few missteps every month, you are actually paying the bank to hold your money.

The low savings rates make it all the more critical to keep as much of your own money in your account and not spend it on bank fees. If you need cash, make it a habit to walk the extra block or drive the extra half-mile to an ATM machine that is in your network. If you don't, you are paying the bank for the use of your money. This is a relatively painless thing you can do to trim spending today—this minute—with virtually no effort.

Seek out fee-free checking accounts at a credit union or bank. The number of free checking accounts being offered dwindles every year. Banks have been slammed by Congress for some of their most lucrative fee-generating practices, so more banks are now charging for small bank accounts instead. You can quickly check and compare bank deposit interest rates at www.bankrate.com. And www.checkingfinder.com offers free and low-cost checking account deals sorted by zip code.

Credit unions are a superb choice for younger savers who don't have a lot of money to deposit. Federal laws protect savings up to $250,000, and credit unions often have less onerous fees and fine print. In the years since the Great Recession, consumers have been shifting to credit unions in huge numbers.[12] You can research credit unions in your area at www.ncua.gov. They are not-for-profit operations, so they are not beholden, as banks are, to shareholders who want to make money from you. They offer auto financing, mortgages, home-equity loans, and other financial services you will likely use in the years ahead. Starting a long relationship with a credit union—and building your three to six months of liquid savings there—is a good early step in your budget plan.

Another great choice is a community bank. Be very clear about what the fees are, and never link your ATM/debit card to the automatic overdraft protection plan. If you do that, you run the risk of big charges when your account runs dry and you overspend. It's always better to walk away without a purchase than pay a $40 surcharge.

Once you figure out where to put your savings, you have to identify other places in the budget to squeeze out some savings.

"All of your bills should be listed, which should include a bill to *yourself* that puts monies into savings," Ryan Mack says. The process of a budget is simple. (I know, I know, budgeting sounds like hard work and scary, but it really is as simple as keeping track of what you eat and how much you exercise. Same concept!) Make a list of what you think you spend every month—housing, cell phone bill, groceries, gas, and tuition or student loan payments. The biggest line item is likely housing, followed by student loans or a car payment. I'm a big believer that young people should live at home after college. Generation X may have regarded living at home as shameful. Not so for millennials. Saving hundreds or thousands of dollars by living at home—especially if you live on the high-cost West Coast or in the Northeast—is the single biggest financial advantage you can give yourself. (More on living at home, renting, and buying a home in Chapter 6.)

Housing costs can be big, but don't overlook the little things: Starbucks, ATM charges, trips to the drugstore, music purchases, and gas and transportation costs. Figure 1.1 shows what a sample budget for millennials should look like.

Certified financial planner Doug Flynn, from Flynn Zito Asset Management, says building wealth and financial success come from having a plan and sticking to it. For 20 years, his clients have used an expense worksheet that

What's coming in?

From job $_____

From parents $_____

What's going out?

Debts

Private student loans $_____

Federal student loans $_____

Extra loan payments $_____

Car payment $_____

Outstanding credit card debt $_____

Family loan $_____

Needs

Housing $_____

Insurance $_____

Groceries $_____

Gas or public transportation $_____

Health care expenses $_____

Phone and Internet (Netflix, etc) $_____

Savings/Investments $_____

Wants

Gym membership* $_____

Coffee/fast food $_____

Apparel $_____

Bars $_____

Recreation (lift tickets, new bike) $_____

Travel (weddings, vacation) $_____

Entertainment (concerts, movie tickets) $_____

Misc 1** $_____

Misc 2** $_____

*Some money managers suggest gym membership is a need, not a want. If you are healthy you will spend less money on health care. But the average annual gym membership is now more than $500. A quick way to save cash is to buy a pair of running shoes and bank the rest.

**Add your own recurring monthly expenses here. Online dating service, financial support you are giving to a family member, or a monthly donation to charity or religious institution.

Figure 1.1   Millennials Sample Budget

helps them track every single penny going out the door. I've simplified it in Figure 1.1 for a more millennial mind-set, with an eye to the fact you are less likely to be a homeowner and more likely to have student loan debt.

Flynn says the goal is to live on 80 percent of what you make, no matter how big or small your income is. The other 20 percent must be allocated for your financial goals—savings and retirement. If you want to give 10 percent to charity, you'll have to live on 70 percent.

Look, it's tough if you are just getting started—and even tougher with student loans on the "liabilities" line of the budget worksheet. You don't go from saving nothing to saving 20 percent overnight.

"You have to begin somewhere. And getting started is the hardest part," Flynn says.

Without savings, you are at extreme risk for building up credit card debt and further delaying your wealth-building goals. Only 51 percent of Americans have more emergency savings than credit card debt, according to Bankrate.com.[13] That is a dangerous statistic. Your savings goal is to be comfortably in the 49 percent of Americans on the right track.

ROADBLOCKS TO MONEY SUCCESS

- "Guesstimating" monthly spending.
- Unrealistic goals.
- Huge student loans, but you don't live like a student.
- Procrastination.
- Paying only minimums on credit cards.

THE HOLIDAY RED FLAG

The most obvious red flag for overspending is something that too many Americans do with ease—and few regrets. Are you still paying off last year's holiday gifts on this year's credit card bill?

Gail Cunningham is a spokesperson for the National Foundation for Credit Counseling (NFCC), and she offers some stark math. Consumers spend on average about $800 on holiday-related expenses—more than a week's wages for a typical worker. "In spite of the fact that the December holidays are an annual event, people routinely neglect planning for them and resort to charging their purchases," she says.[14]

The consumer experience makes it so easy to charge and forget. "Consider the ramifications of this lack of planning," Cunningham says. If a consumer spends $1,000 on a credit card and makes only the minimum monthly payment of 2 percent of the balance with an annual percentage rate of 18 percent, it will take 12 years to pay off the debt.

"The ghost of Christmas past will haunt until 2026," Cunningham adds.

Even assuming no late fees, that $1,000 in holiday spending will have cost you $2,353 by the time you pay it off.

"Buy now, pay later" on high-interest credit cards is a terrible strategy. Whenever you are about to make any purchase, no matter how generous or for which holiday, set your budget, understand what you are spending, and ask yourself with each purchase three simple questions:

1. Do I need this?
2. Will it make me better, smarter, or more prepared?
3. Can I pay this off when my credit card bill comes?

Along those lines, best-selling spiritual guru Deepak Chopra gave me some of the best financial analysis I have ever heard.

"First thing the consumer should learn to do is stop spending money they haven't earned to buy things they don't need to impress people they don't like," Chopra said. "We are buying stuff that we don't need with money that we haven't earned just so we can keep up with the Joneses."

YOUR MONEY QUIZ

So are you one of Chopra's overspending consumers? Answer these questions and find out. Assume you land $10,000 tax-free. What do you do with it?

- Do you put all or some in the bank?
- Do you pay down high-interest credit cards?
- Do you pay down your student loan?
- Do you invest in a traditional or Roth IRA?
- In the past year have you checked your credit report?
- At this very moment, do you know your exact bank balance?

Add up the yes answers

5–6 Overachiever

3–5 Frugalista

1–2 Bubble consumer

0 Not smart. Not rich.

Chapter 1 Action Plan

First, embrace a saver's mentality and begin to map out your plan. Aim for three to six months of living expenses to cover an emergency. Live at home if it will save you big money. If you have large student loan debts, live like it. Don't pay the bank to use your money. Instead, find a low-fee bank account or use a credit union. Never opt in to overdraft protection. Live below your means. Identify waste in your monthly spending and eliminate it. Be ruthless in identifying needs and wants. Every budget, no matter how small, can be trimmed.

College Investment

People have to follow their dreams. If people are interested in art, they should pursue art. If they're interested in business, they should pursue business. But they shouldn't be afraid of numbers and they shouldn't be afraid of things they haven't done before, and they shouldn't be afraid to learn new things.

—Jack Lew, U.S. Secretary of the Treasury

Let's settle the silly "Is college worth it?" debate straightaway. Of course it is. But a college degree costs more than ever, and it doesn't come with the guarantees that it used to.

Face it: You can't afford college. And you can't afford *not* to go to college. The question "Is college worth it?" has become the debate of the twenty-first century. And the answer is yes ... if you are smart about the debt and choose the right major. Once you graduate, you have to manage the debt wisely. Not even bankruptcy will wipe away this debt. It's with you forever until you pay it off.

Let's tackle the debt problem first. There are two schools of thought on education debt in the United States. The first holds that the country is up to its eyeballs in student debt. Student loan balances are now greater than all outstanding credit card debt and second only to mortgage loans. In this camp, there is growing fear that all that debt will keep millennials from marrying, buying homes, and spending money in the economy. The student loan bubble will pop and hurt borrowers and everyone else.

544%

T he jump in tuition since 1985.[1]

The second school of thought can be boiled down to a single headline from the pages of the *New York Times*: "The Reality of Student Loan Debt Is Different from the Clichés."[2] This analysis holds that the typical debt burden per graduate (as a share of their monthly income) has remained relatively steady over the last two decades. This analysis finds that just 7 percent of young-adult households with debt have more than $50,000 of it. The stressed-out bartender with a B.A. and $100,000 in loans is the outlier. The real problem—the true student loan crisis—comes from the graduates who drop out, or take longer than four years to graduate, or pile on graduate school debt for a major that is not rewarded in the economy. For those students, it wasn't worth it. Thankfully, those students are the exception, not the rule.

After a screening of the excellent student debt documentary *Ivory Tower*, in Washington, D.C., a young woman rose to ask a question of a panel I was moderating. "I had $40,000 in student loans and have paid off all but $2,000 of that. It has taken me 6 1/2 years. I drive an old car. I have roommates. But I will pay it off before I am 30," she said. "My question: Are we overhyping the student loan problem?"

Both of these camps are correct; there is a student loan crisis, but it's not as apocalyptic as it sounds. Some graduates, like the young woman in Washington, will pay off their loans in 10 years and turn what they were once paying on the loans into investments for a house or their retirement. However, those who don't find a decent-paying job or those who dropped out and don't have the degree or special skills, unless they take drastic action, will be held back.

Ivory Tower's filmmaker, Andrew Rossi, says the idea of whether college is "worth it" should be more nuanced.

"We can say that statistically a bachelor's degree is worth it, but that does not mean 'college' as a whole is worth it. Sixty-eight percent of students at public institutions do not graduate in four years. Forty-four percent fail to graduate in six years. Those who do not complete and get a degree do not enjoy the wage premium and often are saddled with debt. For nearly half of the people who enter a public four-year institution, the question of whether their experience was 'worth it' is far more complicated," Rossi says.

For the purposes of *Smart Is the New Rich,* the only camp that matters is yours. Just having student debt does not disqualify you from building for the future. That debt—assuming you have not dropped out and you have the degree—is essentially an investment in your future earnings potential. In this chapter we'll explore how to make the most of that investment by keeping the size of the debt down in the first place and choosing the major that is right for you and that will be rewarded in a fast-changing economy. Then in Chapter 3, we'll outline the smart strategies for paying off that debt.

If you don't have debt, you are fortunate. The minute you begin earning money, you can begin saving and investing for the future. Bravo! If you do have debt, you are in good company. Today, 71 percent of those earning a bachelor's degree graduate with debt, which averages $29,400.[3] As Rossi points out, younger graduates skew even higher. Less than a third of graduates make it all the way through on savings, scholarships, and grants. You'll have to live lean and pay down the debt aggressively so it doesn't hold you back.

THE MILLION-DOLLAR PAYOFF

Why do some families save, and some don't? According to Sallie Mae,[4] the families who save for college have a stronger belief that college is a valuable investment and are more willing to stretch themselves financially.

It is eventually a valuable investment. The typical bachelor's degree candidate can expect to earn a million dollars more over the course of a 40-year working life than someone with just a high school degree.[5] Once they get into the labor market after college, the unemployment rate for college graduates is just 3.1 percent.[6]

Those are impressive statistics, but many of you aren't feeling it yet. A recent survey shows millennials are "overwhelmed" by their debts.[7] It's taking them longer to find their first good job, and many are underemployed—working part-time or working in a job far below their skills and education. (More on the job market overall and for millennials in Chapter 4.) Without a decent job, even a small amount of student loan debt can suck too much out of

Table 2.1   Household Income and Assets of College Grads vs. Non–College Grads

	College grad	Non–college grad
Income (median)	$72,800	$34,700
Investable assets	$43,300	$21,600

Source: Wells Fargo Millennial Study, 2014

the monthly budget. Those graduates acutely feel the student debt burden and are aware that it may be holding them back financially for the moment. But here is something amazing about the millennial generation: Three-quarters of millennials who attended college agree that their college education was worth the cost, according to Wells Fargo. Why? As Table 2.1 shows, they will earn more and ultimately have lower unemployment than their noncollege counterparts.

The belief that college is worth it—*eventually*—is why so many families stretch their finances so thin to save for it. A little over half of American families are saving for college,[8] on average putting away $3,398 a year, according to a Sallie Mae survey. So why are so many families *not* saving? Life gets in the way. There are day-to-day bills, retirement planning, a new car, a relative who needs help. It's another reminder, as you plan your own financial life, to adopt healthy habits concerning your debt and pay it down, so you aren't paying off your student loans when you should be saving for your kids' education.

Regardless of income level, Sallie Mae found 9 out of 10 parents value an education as an investment for their child's future. Indeed, more parents are now saving for college, and they are saving more.

REASONS FOR NOT SAVING FOR COLLEGE

- Don't have enough money.
- Belief that scholarships and financial aid will cover it.
- Don't understand their options.
- It's the kid's responsibility.

Source: "How America Saves for College," Sallie Mae

IT'S CHEAPER TO SAVE THAN BORROW

As I mentioned at the start of this chapter, very few people in this country can actually afford college. And that is why many take the attitude that if they don't or can't save, they will get a better shot at student loans and grants. It's not hard to look at the depressing numbers and see why this is a popular path: The cost of tuition is up 544 percent since 1985. Over that same time period, the median household income has only doubled, according to the U.S. Census Bureau. So that means college tuition inflation is outpacing increases in median household income by 5 to 1 in just under 30 years. But saving is always better than borrowing. Every dollar you don't save for tuition will be almost $2 by the time you pay it back. It makes college even more expensive than that sticker price. That's the hard math from student financing expert Mark Kantrowitz, publisher of Edvisors (http://www.edvisors.com), which helps students and parents make decisions about college costs and financial aid, and author of *Filing the FAFSA*.

If your student loan debt is the typical $30,000 at graduation, you could end up paying back much more than that by the time the terms of the loans are done (depending on your interest rates and mix of federal and private loans).

"Even if you start saving very late in the game, you are going to save money," Kantrowitz tells me. "But one of your greatest assets is time. If you start saving from the year the child is born, about a third of your savings goal will come from the earnings [on the investment]. If you wait until the child enters high school, less than 10 percent of your savings goal will come from earnings."

Bottom line, if your parents saved for your college, you owe them a huge debt of gratitude.

If they didn't, you'll have to make the very most out of the investment by keeping the debt down.

If step 1 in the college investment is saving for it, then step 2 is choosing the right school and knowing what you are paying for. College is so expensive now and so many people get loans to pay for it that the total price becomes meaningless. The numbers in Table 2.2 are enormous. The College Board keeps the official stats on education costs and found that a four-year

Table 2.2   College Costs

College	Public 4-year in-state	Private nonprofit 4-year
Total Charges	$18,391	$40,917

Source: College Board, 2013 College Pricing report

education at an in-state public school costs on average $18,391 per year. At private universities, the cost jumps to $40,917 a year. It's almost funny money for someone who has never had a paycheck and is leaving home. It's hard for anyone to really get their head around these kinds of numbers. There's another way to look at the numbers. If you drill down to how much that education costs each week you are physically in school, it comes to $613 a week for a public in-state college and $1,363 a week for a private school. These numbers, of course, are the average, and they are the sticker price. The price will be lower after applying grants, scholarships, and loans. Mark Kantrowitz urges families to focus on the "net price" of the education, not the "net cost."

Net price is what you pay after accounting for any grant money, scholarships, or gift aid money that doesn't need to be repaid. Kantrowitz calls it the "discounted sticker price"—the amount a family will have to pay from savings, income, and loans to cover the college cost. "It is a much better basis for comparing the cost for colleges," Kantrowitz says. Don't be lulled into thinking those loans the financial aid office is helping you arrange are going to make the tuition more manageable. Those loans will make the cost of the education *higher* in the end.

But there are steps to take to help keep your college costs down. Start with these.

FOUR WAYS TO KEEP COLLEGE COSTS DOWN

Number 1: *Pick a college you can afford.* Young people have been led to believe they can afford a Mercedes education on a Honda budget. It's simply not true. Saddling a young person with tens of thousands of dollars in debt in the name of getting a degree from the "right" school is insane. Pure and simple. The good news is that behaviors are changing. A study by Sallie Mae found 69 percent of families are now ruling out colleges that are too expensive. Students are evaluating housing costs on campus and signing up when they can for cheaper, leaner dorm rooms. This alone could begin to put the brakes on that insane 544 percent rise in tuition since 1985.

Financial aid guru Kantrowitz says too often students are "chasing a dream." They want to go to a school with a great reputation or with the best name in their field. "They figure they'll figure out how to pay for the debt after they graduate, but the time to reduce your debt is before you incur it, not afterwards," Kantrowitz says. "You don't need to go to the most expensive and least generous college in the country to get a high quality education."

He adds a new category to the perennial college wish list. In addition to a "reach" school, two good matches, and a safety school, he recommends students add a "financial safety school—a college that will not only admit you but where you attend even with no financial aid." Yes, that is what it has come to. The lofty pursuit of education and knowledge has a price tag that is simply too high.

In the face of such expenses, many millennials are choosing to start out at a community college, where tuition is far lower, and then transfer to a state or private college to finish their degree. This is possible because of the partnerships—or articulation agreements—many colleges and universities have with community colleges in their region. Check out http://www.finaid.org/otheraid/partnerships.phtml as a good place to start for more on these partnerships. Students taking this route may have even more options. In late 2013, 27 public and private colleges and universities ranging from Auburn University to Ohio State and Gonzaga University said they would join the first national network of two- and four-year academic institutions. So the community college route is becoming more attractive.

There are other creative options to keep costs down. Blackburn College in Illinois is one of a handful of four-year colleges in the country that keeps tuition costs lower by requiring all students to work at least 10 hours a week on campus. The work experience translates on the resume later, and keeps student loan debt down. To see my video story about Blackburn College.

http://www.cnn.com/video/?/video/cnnmoney/2014/11/14 /ivory-dorm.cnnmoney&video_referrer=http%3A%2F%2Fwww .cnn.com%2FSPECIALS%2Fus%2Fcnn-film-ivory-tower%2Findex .html

Number 2: *Graduate in four years.* Long gone are the days of "finding yourself" and the five-year bachelor's degree. If you are paying for school with student loans, under no circumstances can you take a semester off or drop out. It's the worst financial decision you'll ever make in your life. For particularly ambitious students, a three-year degree is advisable. Some universities offer three-year programs for dedicated students, and a growing list of universities have made pledges to hold down tuition for middle-class students. For a list of the schools offering financial aid packages with no loans or limited loans, go to www.projectonstudentdebt.org. (It's a diverse list, including Arizona State University, Emory University, Oberlin College, University of California, and Yale University, among others.) In-state tuition at public universities is one of the best education values out there (though tuition for them is rising quickly, too). Acquire College Level Examination Program (CLEP) and Advanced Placement (AP) course credits in high school to transfer with you as a freshman. And consider getting first-year math and reading requirements out of the way at a community college while you are still in high school to help you graduate in four years. This is essential, especially if you go to a big in-state public school where there can be difficulty getting the required classes out of the way in the first couple of years.

Number 3: *Speak STEM.* The acronym STEM (Science, Technology, Engineering, Math) represents the corner of the economy that is growing jobs and creating exciting new careers and opportunities. Eight of the ten top-earning careers are in engineering. The highest-paid graduates among English majors are technical writers. Whatever the major, translate those skills for that growing part of the economy. Consider a STEM minor or a double degree. "If you are pursuing a field of study you know doesn't pay very well you need to borrow less or double major with a second major in a field that can pay the rent after you graduate," Kantrowitz advises. "It's one thing to pursue your dreams but presumably if you are borrowing to pay for your education you want to be able to have enough income to repay those student loans."

Number 4: *Live like a student.* When you are in college, keep the spending to a minimum. Student loans are not meant to be used for spring break or new clothes. After college, if you have student loans, the advice is the same. Live like a student. Remember, every dollar you spend will be two dollars you'll have to pay back later.

WHAT DO YOU WANT TO BE WHEN YOU GROW UP?

In reporting on the value of a college education, I am often confronted with conflicting messages from employers and academics. Many CEOs complain that college graduates just are not ready for the workforce. They see indebted students with no work experience but with expensive educations. They see young, tech-savvy college graduates who don't know how to apply that education to the fast-growing and quickly changing corners of the economy. But professors and university presidents (especially at traditional liberal arts colleges) bristle at the notion of college being a training ground for corporate jobs. They see their role as teaching students how to learn, think, and create. Those qualities contribute the problem solving and innovation that define the U.S. economy. Education is for the sake of learning and exploration, not for job training. I see both points. But from your perspective, as the consumer of the college education and the applicant in the workforce, the question in higher education is not just "What do you want to major in?" Today, the practical question is "What do you want to major in that someone will pay you for?"

The old question "What do you want to be when you grow up?" is really three questions:

1. What are you naturally good at?
2. What do you like to do?
3. What will someone pay you for?

Where the answers to those three questions intersect is where you should focus your college investment. If your passion is basketball but you are not LeBron James, what careers can you see yourself doing that deal with basketball, be it advertising, media or production, marketing, or training? A good exercise is to draw a wheel with spokes (see Figure 2.1). In the center, write

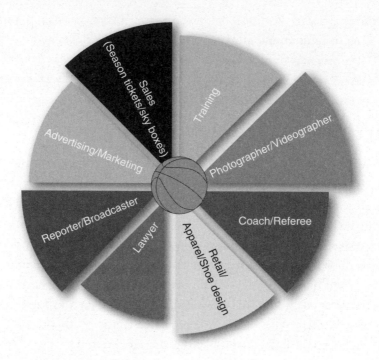

Figure 2.1   Passion Wheel

what your passion is and then at the end of those spokes, write the careers you can build around that passion and the skills and training required to get there.

Everyone excels at what they are passionate about. So you need to find this yourself and understand what it takes to be able to work in that field. I'd never recommend that someone pursue engineering who didn't like math. I wouldn't suggest a career in the hard sciences if your passion lies elsewhere. But I do suggest that an art history student minor in statistics or business or marketing.

At the beginning of this chapter, I quoted Treasury Secretary Jack Lew. The context of that quote is critical. He was addressing a group of business leaders in San Francisco who were concerned that today's college graduates do not have the appropriate math, engineering, and technical skills to meet the demand for jobs. They were concerned about the "skills gap" between what companies need and what college graduates have to offer. They need workers who are literate and *numerate*—unintimidated by numbers and able to distill data and make decisions based on them. I interviewed Lew after that encounter with business leaders and asked him to elaborate on his admonition that college students be more focused on the skills companies need. He wanted to make very clear to young people that the best of this country is its academic diversity and the skills taught through a pursuit of liberal arts. It's not one or the other, he told me, it's both: math and numbers affinity and a broad-based liberal arts–rich education. He wasn't ready yet to say that America needs millions of number crunchers or computer geniuses.

Ask the same question of a tech company CEO and the answer is quite different. I have asked dozens of tech company CEOs and venture capitalists this question: "What do you recommend high school seniors should be when they grow up?"

STEM. STEM. STEM and STEM. Not a single person has told me journalism or French (my double major).

Scott Sullivan, the senior vice president of people operations at Motorola in Chicago, answers that question with one word and a slight, knowing smile: "Engineering."

Eric Schmidt, the chairman of Google, told me he could hire an unlimited number of "10X" engineers if only the United States were creating enough of them. The term *10X* is used in tech land to refer to the rock-star programmers who outcode and outprogram everyone else. They are, essentially, 10 times as valuable as the typical (overachieving) engineer. Schmidt told me my kids should be coding as soon as they show interest. (In fact, he challenged me when I told him I use the video game Minecraft as a reward to my son for practicing the piano. He said I had it backward. "If your son excels at Minecraft, let him code!").

There are other technical skills CEOs value, not just coding. The founder and CEO of FedEx, Fred Smith, told me the traditional four-year bachelor's degree isn't for everyone, and for the jobs he's hiring for it's a waste of money compared with a high school degree and post–high school training.

"I think you'll find that there are a lot of positions like that, like the crane operators for container ships on the West Coast making $150,000," Smith said.

"What's going on in the country, in many places including our headquarters in the city and surrounding areas, there's a tremendous influence of employer interface with community college, where the community colleges are actually putting in place a curriculum to meet local needs. And in our case it's aviation, maintenance technicians, IT repair folks, and those are terrific jobs for people with high school educations who go to local community college," said Smith, who noted that an aviation mechanic makes $100,000 midcareer.

I'm quite bullish on community colleges eventually becoming an important pipeline with companies to deliver the skills they need with a smaller investment than the traditional B.A. or B.S. degree from a four-year college. It is an important consideration in the "Is college worth it?" debate. A list of the community colleges with the highest-earning graduates can be found in the appendix.

I encourage you to check out community college apprenticeship programs. I profiled Apprenticeship2000 in North Carolina, where students are paid to go to college. You can see my video story here:

http://www.cnn.com/video/?/video/cnnmoney/2014/11/14/ivory-apprentice.cnnmoney&video_referrer=http%3A%2F%2Fwww.cnn.com%2FSPECIALS%2Fus%2Fcnn-film-ivory-tower%2Findex.html

Of course, a big part of the student loan crisis is the huge number of students who are entering college without the skills they need to succeed. The studies vary, but show anywhere from 28 percent to 40 percent of college freshman are taking remedial math and English their first year. At $18,000 to $40,000 a year, that is a huge waste of money for something that should have been learned in high school. The billionaire U.S. investor Wilbur Ross told me he worries that U.S. public school students are entering college unprepared for the course material and for the world. Yet his advice for young people deciding what they want to be when they grow up? "You should be the real you and comfortable with being yourself. Playacting only works in theaters and often fails even there. It never succeeds for long in real life."

In other words, you can't play the role of computer programmer if you have a love of comparative literature. And business school won't suit you if you hate it. The trick is finding that intersection of what you are good at, what you like to do, and what the economy favors.

NOT ALL DEGREES ARE EQUAL

The major you choose and the degree you hold matter. Georgetown University's Center on Education and the Workforce crunches the numbers on college majors and subsequent employment and finds that not all degrees are created equal.[9] Georgetown researchers call it a "harsh reality" that even though a college degree gives job seekers "a formidable advantage over those without," recent college graduates bear most of the risk in a very lopsided market for their degrees and talents.

No surprise, engineering dominates the list of stable and growing occupations and offers excellent pay. Jobless rates for recent graduates are relatively low, and recent engineering graduates can expect $51,000 to $57,000 a year to start. The unemployment rate for engineering graduates is anywhere from 2.3 to 3.1 percent, and the pay scale ranges from $95,000 to $109,000. Table 2.3 details the jobless rates and earnings for engineering graduates.

Jobless rates are also low in health care, and demand is exploding for jobs up and down the income ladder. A word of warning: Many of the fastest-growing jobs in health care are for home health care workers and health care aides, which do not require a college degree and for which pay is only $19,000 to $20,000 a year. But overall, Georgetown finds that health care is a growing and lucrative field. (Indeed, the U.S. Department of Labor

Table 2.3 Jobless Rates and Earnings for Engineering Graduates

Major	Recent grad jobless rate	Experienced grad jobless rate	Grad degree jobless rate	Recent grad earnings	Experienced grad earnings	Grad degree earnings
General Engineering	7.0%	4.8%	2.3%	$55,000	$77,000	$98,000
Chemical Engineering		3.1%	2.8%		$94,000	$102,000
Civil Engineering	7.6%	4.0%	3.1%	$51,000	$81,000	$95,000
Electrical Engineering	7.6%	4.6%	3.0%	$57,000	$91,000	$109,000
Mechanical Engineering	8.1%	3.4%	2.9%	$57,000	$86,000	$101,000
Electrical Engineering Technology			5.7%		$70,000	
Industrial Production Technologies		2.5%			$70,000	

Source: Center on Education and the Workforce, Georgetown University

Table 2.4   Jobless Rates and Earnings for Health Care Graduates

Health majors	Recent grad jobless rate	Experienced grad jobless rate	Grad degree jobless rate	Recent college grad earnings	Experienced college grad earnings	Grad degree earnings
General Medical and Health Services		3.9%			$56,000	
Health and Medical Administrative Services		4.6%			$55,000	
Medical Technologies Technicians		2.8%			$61,000	
Nursing	4.8%	2.3%	1.7%	$48,000	$65,000	$81,000
Pharmacy Pharmaceutical Sciences and Administration		2.5%	2.9%		$180,000	$110,000
Treatment Therapy Professions		2.1%			$65,000	

Source: Center on Education and the Workforce, Georgetown University

consistently ranks health care among the fastest-growing job categories.) Table 2.4 shows the jobless rate for recent nursing graduates, for example, at around 4.8 percent, with a $48,000 salary.

As the baby boomers age and technology drives more consumption of high-tech medical care, there will be a huge demand for wellness occupations, podiatry, and occupational and physical therapy. (More on potential growth in these fields in Chapter 4.)

Once they get into the workforce, education majors enjoy more job stability but comparatively low pay. Frankly, I believe that for the importance of this profession pay should be higher. This is a critical question for U.S. policy makers and voters going forward. Children in the United States are in school only a little more than 180 days a year and are off for more than two months in the summer, resulting in an annual "summer slide," during which up to 40 percent of what they learned during the year is lost. Public education should have a longer school year and higher pay for teachers. The United States won't lead the world in the twenty-first century unless more of its children are entering college ready for the work. According to college testing company ACT, only 26 percent of incoming freshmen are ready for college in all four testing subjects—English, math, reading, and science.[10]

Clearly, the United States should be investing in good teachers at the front of a classroom for far more school days. In China, the public school year is 35 days longer than it is here. U.S. Secretary of Education Arne Duncan has long argued for longer school days and longer school years. And he thinks teachers should be compensated well for it. He told me he thinks great teachers should make six figures.

"We should be rewarding excellence. We should be encouraging teachers to go to work in the most underserved communities. Let me be clear—no teacher ever goes into education to make a million dollars. I've been very public. I think starting teachers' salaries should be much higher. I think a great teacher should be able to make, pick a number, $120, $130, $150,000 a year," Duncan says.

As you can see in Table 2.5, teacher salaries would have to be tripled to get there.

Researchers at Georgetown's Center on Education and the Workforce conclude:

> In the past a college degree all but assured job seekers [would] find employment and high earnings. But today, what you make depends on what you take....STEM—Science, Technology, Engineering,

Table 2.5   Education Major Earnings and Unemployment Rates

Education major	Recent grad jobless rate	Experienced grad jobless rate	Grad degree jobless rate	Recent grad earnings	Experienced grad earnings	Grad degree earnings
General	7.6%	4.2%	2.8%	$34,000	$43,000	$56,000
Elementary	5.0%	3.7%	1.4%	$33,000	$41,000	$55,000
Physical and Health		4.1%	2.6%		$49,000	$65,000
Early Childhood		5.5%			$39,000	
Secondary Teacher		3.6%			$46,000	
Special Needs		4.5%	1.9%		$45,000	$58,000
Language and Drama		4.6%	12.3%		$44,000	$58,000
Art and Music		3.9%			$45,000	
Misc.		3.1%			$50,000	

Source: Center on Education and the Workforce, Georgetown University

and Mathematics—majors typically offer the best opportunities for employment and earnings, while unemployment is higher for graduates with non-technical degrees.[11]

It bears repeating, what you make depends on what you take. As you can see from Table 2.6 not all degrees are created equal when it comes to the unemployment line. The college degree is still the golden ticket, but where and how you punch it is key. In some fields, the unemployment rate is lower but in others it will take longer to pay off loans. Bankrate.com, a personal finance website, found that in many fields where jobs are being created, pay is high and graduate degrees are not necessary.[12]

- Typical salaries for advertising/marketing/promotions specialists can top $100,000, and no graduate degree is necessary. Typical workers in this area can pay off their student loans in as little as six years.
- Economists should be able to pay back their loans in 7.1 years, Bankrate estimates. Median salary is $92,000, and they have a below-average degree cost of $53,000.
- Civil engineers are set for student loan debt freedom in as little as 8.5 years. Median salary is a healthy $80,000, and the cost of the degree is below average.
- Although doctors earn a comfortable salary on average ($172,020), the extra years in school cost them. According to Bankrate.com analysis, it should take almost 11 years for doctors to pay off their student loans.
- Lawyers, teachers, and journalists better love what they do, especially if they borrowed money to get a degree. Bankrate found the typical lawyer will not pay back loans for 13 years. Journalists and teachers will

Table 2.6   Highest/Lowest Jobless Rates by Major

Lowest unemployment rate	Highest unemployment rate
Nursing 4.8%	Political Science 11.1%
Elementary Education 5.0%	Film, Video, and Photography Arts 11.4%
Physical Fitness, Parks and Recreation 5.2%	Anthropology 12.6%
Chemistry 5.8%	Architecture 12.8%
Finance 5.9%	Information Systems 14.7%

Source: Center on Education and the Workforce, Georgetown University

take considerably longer. Median pay is between $37,000 and $43,000, leaving little room for hefty student loan payments. If 10 percent of their pay is budgeted for student loans each year, it will take journalists about 32 years to pay them off, and teachers 22 years.

Chapter 2 Action Plan

The numbers are numbing, but they don't lie: College is worth it. So start saving for it if you haven't already, and live like a student who is in debt, not using loans for trips or clothes. Remember, every dollar you don't save for tuition will be worth almost $2 by the time you pay it back. Map out what your passion is, and brainstorm about how you can build a career around it. More power (and money!) to you if it's in a field related to STEM (Science, Technology, Engineering, Math) fields. Then pick a college you can afford. Weigh the options of a community college versus jumping right into an expensive four-year university. And—for your wallet's sake—don't take more than four years to finish college.

Managing Debt

37% ━━━━━━━━━━━━━━━━━━━━━━━━━━━━━━━━━

Share of adults under 40 years old with some student debt—a record high. The median outstanding debt: $13,000.[1]

━━

All college graduates have an automatic job the minute they receive their diploma: They become their own financial manager. Two-thirds of college graduates finish with some level of student loan debt. Paying it off quickly and aggressively is job one.

Funny thing is, when they borrowed the money for college, most people did not receive much guidance about how to pay it back. Student loan debt can't be forgotten or delayed. It follows you forever. It is rarely forgiven in bankruptcy. If you don't make payments on the loans, it will hurt your credit score and damage your chances of renting an apartment, buying a house, or leasing a car. If you have private student loans, your family could be responsible for them if you die prematurely.

Student loan debt is so permanent, so unforgiving—if you don't pay it off today, the government could someday garnish your Social Security check. Millennials are some four decades away from receiving Social Security, so they may not find this so alarming. But their parents will. In 2013, 156,000 Americans had their Social Security checks garnished because they had outstanding student loans on which they defaulted. That number has more than tripled, from 47,500 in 2006.[2]

Life *only* gets more complicated in the years after college. So paying student loans off aggressively now, before marriage, homeownership, and kids, is the best strategy for most young people. You may not be a student anymore, but living with student debt means living like a student.

> Living with student debt means living like a student.

I know that advice is depressing and not very popular among some of your peers. Sometimes the pile of debt is just so big, it loses all meaning. Many millennials get debt fatigue. They are scrimping and saving every month, and it doesn't look like they are making a dent in their bills.

And most likely, it's not just the student loans you are juggling. Pew Research found that young people with student loans were more likely to have car loans and credt card debt, too.[3]

Here is that four-letter word again: *time*. The longer the period that good habits rule your finances, the better off you are in the longer term.

No one is asking you to live like a monk, but you've got to live within reason financially.

"It's a necessity today: how to balance student loan debt with future goals," says Ameriprise executive vice president Pat O'Connell. "It's having a conversation with people about not carrying balances from month to month. Be careful about how much rent or mortgage debt you take on. And on the asset side, it's about building a foundation with a cash reserve and taking advantage of your company's 401(k) plan."

If you can't afford it, don't put it on a credit card—it's the worst sort of high-interest debt that will hold you back. (More on managing credit and credit cards in Chapter 9.)

You simply must be saving for the future, even as you are paying off the past.

Stephanie Genkin, an independent fee-only financial planner based in Brooklyn, told me she advises her clients to keep the student debt front and center on the balance sheet. Paying it down must be the first priority. "Those paying back $500 or more a month must realize there is a huge opportunity cost," Genkin says. "It will affect how they live, whether they can afford to buy a home (barring help from family) and it will take a bite out of what they are able to save for emergencies (putting many at the mercy of credit cards with high interest rates if things go wrong)."

Student Debt Is Forever

- It is rarely forgiven in bankruptcy.
- Missed payments hurt your credit score.
- Private student loans survive even if you die.
- Wages and Social Security checks can be garnished.

PAYING OFF THE DEBT

If you haven't figured it out by now, this is the tough-love chapter of the book. But the key message here is that there is a way through the morass of student debt. So let's break down the various kinds of debt and how to deal with them.

There are four kinds of student debtors:

1. The graduate who cannot sleep at night knowing the debt is there. This graduate lives at home or with friends, rarely eats out (or scours the landscape for good deals), and pays every single available penny toward the loans.
2. The graduate who accepts this debt as the cost of doing business and automatically pays the minimum every month, allowing the interest to grow and accepting the debt as the background noise of postcollege life.
3. The graduate who just forgets about the debt and quickly defaults.
4. The unfortunate soul who quit college without a degree but still has the student loans to pay back. The personal student debt load may well shut this person out of the middle class.

The first two on this list have a real shot at building for the future even as they are paying off the past. Student loan debt does not preclude you from organizing your bills and making investments. It just takes careful prioritizing.

The last thing you want is a relatively small, unplanned expense (fixing a cracked iPhone screen, a friend's last-minute destination wedding, new tires for your car) throwing you into high-interest credit card debt and derailing your careful debt strategy.

And, of course, since you have such a long time horizon, you'll want to begin investing as soon as possible. (Jump ahead to Chapter 8 if your high-interest debt is paid off and you're ready to have fun beginning your investments.) If you're not there yet, here's a good approach:

1. *Map out your strategy.*

    Understand how long it will take to pay off your student loans. Bankrate.com has a helpful calculator, and your student loan servicer most likely has this information readily available as well.

    http://www.bankrate.com/finance/student-loans/how-long-to-pay-off-student-loan.aspx

    Fidelity Investments offers five critical steps for managing your debts and investing, too. You can find this information at https://www.fidelity.com/viewpoints/personal-finance/how-to-pay-off-debt.

2. *Set aside money for an emergency.*[4]

    Fidelity recommends three to six months of living expenses set aside to prevent even worse financial stress if your car breaks down or you lose your job. For single people, three months may be enough, but young families should set aside enough money for at least six months. Trying to build it slowly? Fidelity suggests setting up automatic payments from your paycheck or checking account into a separate account as an emergency fund. Make sure there are no fees for low balances.

3. *Don't pass up the match.*

    The company 401(k) match at work is free money. One of the biggest money mistakes young people make is thinking they shouldn't invest in a 401(k) at work until they are debt-free. Here's the Fidelity math on this: Imagine your company contributes 50 cents for every $1 you contribute, up to 3 percent of your salary. If you make $60,000 a year and contribute 3 percent, or $1,800 a year, your company puts $900 right into the account, too, for a yearly total of $2,700. Do that every year for 10 years, and Fidelity says the $2,700 a year will be worth $37,000, assuming a 7 percent average rate of return.

4. *Pay this debt first: high-interest credit card balances.*

As a society, we have made it way too easy for people to live way beyond their means on credit cards. And it is so easy to amass a big pile of high-interest debt. The system is rigged to keep you in debt and reap huge interest and fee charges once you fall behind. Under no circumstances can you just pay the minimum amount each month and get out of that debt quickly. This is the pile to chip away at before you pay extra on your student loans.

Here's what Fidelity recommends to its clients: Avoid using a credit card to finance purchases. Why? In some cases it could double the cost of the purchase. A dollar borrowed to buy something on a credit card is far more than a dollar paid back in the end. Fidelity uses the example of a $2,000 TV financed with a credit card with a 15 percent interest rate. If you make only the $40 minimum payment each month, it would take you more than 17 years to pay off that television. The TV will be long gone by the time you pay it off, and you would have paid $2,500 in interest—more than the original cost of the television. Crazy! (More on managing credit card debt and burnishing the credit score in Chapter 9.)

5. *Pay private student loans.*

Private loans carry higher interest rates than government student loans, ranging from 5 percent to 12 percent, which can be more than double the rate for government student loans. Fidelity notes that you may be able to deduct the interest on a student loan, but only up to $2,500 a year if you are a single filer earning less than $75,000 a year. Fidelity urges that you use this rule of thumb: It's a good idea to pay down student debt above 8 percent interest. This is especially true when this debt is not tax-deductible.

6. *Contribute more to the 401(k).*

With high-interest credit card debt paid off and private loans paid down, it's time to beef up the 401(k) investing.

Here's what Fidelity advises its clients: "While you may still have a government student loan, car loan, or a mortgage, these loans typically have much lower interest rates. That's why it can make sense to bump up your 401(k) contributions and continue to make payments on these loans."

Here's the math on a bigger contribution. Contribute 10 percent, or $6,000 a year on a $60,000 salary, and the company would add $900. Do that for 10 years and that $6,900 a year could grow to more than $95,000, assuming a rate of 7 percent a year, according to Fidelity.

7. *Pay the monthly minimums on government student loans, car loans, or mortgages.*

These debts have tax benefits and low interest rates, so it's fine to pay the minimums on these each month.

INTEREST RATE TRIAGE

Essentially, you should organize your debts from highest interest rate to lowest, and consider the tax ramifications of each of them. On very low-interest-rate loans, it makes sense to make the minimum payments, especially if the interest is tax-deductible. A car loan at 3 percent should not be paid (beyond the minimum) if you can be diverting more money to the 401(k). Mortgage interest is tax-deductible and mortgage rates are near record lows. There was a long-held rule of thumb that you should make one extra mortgage payment a year to pay down the mortgage loan faster. But with the stock market rising and mortgage rates near record lows, that rule of thumb does not hold true for the first time in generations! And, frankly, mortgage debt is not a huge issue for millennials, who overwhelmingly prefer living at home or renting.

Here is the order to follow to triage your debt:

1. *Pay this!* If you have private student loans at higher than an 8 percent interest rate, it makes sense to prioritize those above other, lower-interest debts.

2. *Get advice on this!* For other student loan debts, the situation is less clear. In some cases, it makes sense to pay down medium-interest-rate debt such as Direct PLUS and Direct Unsubsidized loans for graduate students. Here's a great example where a visit with a fee-only financial

planner can help you organize the debts that are best for your tax situation, financial goals, and appetite for risk.

3. *Pay the minimum on this!* Interest rates are so low on some of these debts, it makes sense to make the minimum monthly payment only. Low-interest Direct loans for undergraduates and Perkins loans or medium-interest-rate loans that are tax-deductible don't need to be paid down.[5] (Again, you must pay the minimums on these loans.)

---

10 YEARS

If you can't pay student loan debt in a decade, you need an alternate payment plan.

A SAFETY NET FOR LOW-INCOME GRADS

The goal is to pay student loan debt back in 10 years or less.

If your total student debt is less than your first year's salary, in theory you should be able to pay it off and move on sometime around your thirtieth birthday. As you learned in Chapter 2, it depends on how much money you make in your field after graduation.

"If your debt exceeds your annual income, you're probably struggling to make those loan payments and you'll probably need an alternate repayment plan like income based repayment," or you need to stretch out the length of the loan so the monthly payments are lower, says student loan expert Mark Kantrowitz of Edvisors.

Indeed, there is relief of sorts for college graduates drowning in this student loan debt.

Income-based repayment (IBR)—and its more recent iteration, President Barack Obama's Pay as You Earn—are the safety nets for low-earning graduates who have above-average student loan debt.

"If you can't afford to repay your student loans on a ten-year repayment plan, Income Based Repayment is a good option because it bases your monthly payment on a percentage of your discretionary income," says Kantrowitz.

Here's how it works. Under IBR, monthly student loan bills are capped at 15 percent of your discretionary income, and whatever debt is left over is forgiven after 25 years. Pay As You Earn caps your student loan payments each month at 10 percent of your disposable income. After 20 years, if you still have student loan debt, the federal government forgives it.

Who qualifies? It's for federal student loans only, and in 2014 an executive order by President Obama expanded the program to include 5 million more borrowers who took out loans before October 2007 or stopped borrowing by October 2011.

For more on income-based repayment, visit www.ibrinfo.org

The government provides this calculator to run the numbers and see which program is right for you: https://studentloans.gov/myDirectLoan/mobile/repayment/repaymentEstimator.action

The goal, says Kantrowitz, is "to make sure the debt doesn't hang over your head for the rest of your life."

There's a way to magnify the benefits of IBR. It's a smart tactic financial planner Stephanie Genkin uses with her high-debt, low-pay millennial clients. Since IBR is based on a percentage of a graduate's adjusted gross income (AGI), it makes sense to reduce that AGI by contributing to a company 401(k), a 403(b), or a traditional individual retirement account (IRA).

"It (is) a no-brainer really," Genkin says. "My clients who are enrolled in IBR are able to pay less on their student loan each month when they contribute to a qualified pre-tax retirement account. It's an even better deal when they get an employer match. Then they can't afford *not* to sock money away for retirement because they are getting free money (not to mention the growth over decades)."

There's also the morale boost of watching your investments grow.

"Contributing monthly to a tax deferred retirement plan helps young debt-burdened clients reduce the psychological fatigue that comes with paying back huge sums of money over time," says Genkin. "They're not just throwing money down the black hole with nothing to show for it. They are building something for their future."

One word of caution from Genkin: This might not be the way to go for every student with low income and high debt. Critics charge that IBR forces the borrower to shell out a lot more money in the long run, since reduced monthly payments are spread out over a longer period of time and therefore accrue more interest.

PUBLIC SERVICE LOAN FORGIVENESS

If you work full-time in a public service job, you may qualify for debt forgiveness. This is a program passed by Congress in 2007 to help ease the burden of skyrocketing tuition costs and to encourage students to enter low-paying but socially important fields such as military service, law enforcement, public education, and public health. Full-time employees of certain nonprofit organizations also qualify. Pay on time every month for 10 years while employed in public service, and the remaining student loan debt can be forgiven after 10 years. There's a lot of fine print about who qualifies, which types of loans are forgiven, and whether to consolidate federal loans. If this is you—working at a nonprofit, in public health, legal aid, law enforcement, or education—it pays to navigate the rules and contact your federal student loan servicer for more details.

The federal government's consumer watchdog, the Consumer Financial Protection Bureau (CFPB), estimates that 25 percent of the U.S. workforce is employed in public service work and may qualify for debt forgiveness programs. Whether it is IBR or another loan forgiveness program, it pays to spend the time looking into it and understand your options.

For more on student loan forgiveness from the CFPB and the Department of Education, go to:

www.consumerfinance.gov/askcfpb/641/what-public-service-loan-forgiveness.html

http://studentaid.ed.gov/publicservice

http://files.consumerfinance.gov/f/201308_cfpb_pledge-action-guide-for-employees.pdf

LIVE LIKE A STUDENT

Ubiquitous student loan debt is the background noise for the millennial generation. Many young people accept it as part of their generation's shared experience. Young people tell me they don't judge someone with a lot of student loan debt, and they try to pay monthly installments, forget about it, and live their lives. Thirty-year-old Nick, in California, says his generation views student loan debt as the norm.

"I don't believe it is a bad thing when it can be considered an investment," he says. "If it vastly increases your earning potential then it is a no-brainer. That isn't always the case and should be considered when deciding [on your] school/major."

Nick is pursuing an advanced degree in physics and is borrowing the money to do it. And as you learned in Chapter 2, STEM education is in hot demand right now. Nick's borrowing is clearly an investment, not a liability,

Nick has a healthy attitude to a degree, but be very careful about becoming blasé.

- Live within your means.
- Don't carry credit card balances.
- Pay more than the student loan minimum.
- Contribute to a tax-advantaged retirement plan.

"I come across many people who feel entitled to live like they don't have debt because somehow student loan debt is acceptable," says Stephanie Genkin. "That's not the reality when you have $50,000 of outstanding education loans at 6 percent interest. You should not feel entitled to upgrade your lifestyle until it's paid off."

Sometimes the alphabet soup of repayment programs and different types of loans can seem overwhelming. Add in credit card debt and the costs of trying to get started in life, and many young people say they just don't feel as if they can get a handle on the scope of their financial obligations. Or they feel the loan balance is just so big, it doesn't even make a dent in their financial picture to put a little more on the credit card or let a few bills slide. Some students tell me that college is a once-in-a-lifetime opportunity and they don't want to downgrade their standard of living just because their parents couldn't save enough. They want to enjoy college (and the years right after) just as their friends do.

This is a messy and costly mind-set. Think of your debt as a part-time job, to be managed and worked on. You'll spend hours checking with income-based repayment options—or student debt forgiveness programs if you work in public service or for a nonprofit—and you'll need to stay in constant contact with your lenders. Autopay your loans each month to secure a lower interest rate if possible, and always contact your loan provider immediately if you move.

Excellent advice from the Project on Student Debt: Lower your principal if you can. Try to pay more than the minimum on the loan, and assign the difference to principal, not to interest. Attach a written request to the lender with the extra payment, and keep track of it. Paying extra on the principal will lower the amount of interest you pay off over time.

The Project on Student Debt has a helpful checklist for recent graduates at this website: http://projectonstudentdebt.org/recent_grads.vp.html

Here's a condensed version: It's critical that you know what type of loans you have and how the grace periods differ. Research the repayment options. The standard payback period is 10 years. If you stretch your payments beyond that, you will pay thousands more in interest. Learn your options in the event of severe financial setback. There are deferments and forbearance to hit the pause button on your payments, but interest will keep racking up—so know your options.[6]

Delinquency and default are devastating to your credit score. If you're not making your federal student loan payments, you're in default after nine months. The total loan balance is instantly due, and the government can (and will) garnish your wages and tax refunds. Defaulting on your obligations is a financial nuclear bomb.

Chapter 3 Action Plan

Think of your debt as a part-time job. Do not let it become simply background noise—actively look for ways to ease the burden. Investing a little in a tax-advantaged retirement account can lower your AGI and lower your monthly student loan payment if you are in an income-based repayment plan. Arrange other bills by interest rate and tax benefit, and follow your strategy for whittling them down. Beware of debt fatigue: Pay your bills on time, every time—or you will blow up your credit rating and severely limit your options down the road. IBR programs for student loans and debt forgiveness programs for public service employees depend on a track record of paying the bills every month. If you are in college on loans, or living after college with student debt, you must live like a student. Keep the costs down and focus on the important things: the new phone you want, a friend's wedding, or an occasional nice dinner.

CHAPTER

Job Market Fundamentals

2

There are two job seekers for every available position. This is the best ratio since before the Great Recession.[1]

The job market is getting better. It really is. At the worst of the Great Recession, there were seven job seekers for each open job in the United States. Today that number is less than two, meaning statistically you only have to beat out one other person to nab the job.

In the sea of economic statistics, that number is quite encouraging. The recovery in jobs, though slow and not yet broad-based, is more important to you today than just about any other economic statistic—more crucial than the stock market rally, the price of coffee, the interest rate on your student loan, or any other number in your financial life.

Unless you have a trust fund (lucky you!) or you just sold a high-frequency trading algorithm right out of school to Goldman Sachs (don't spend it all in one place!), your job is the engine of your personal economy. The job brings a paycheck; it pays the bills and fuels the savings and investments that will carry you into ever more exciting stages of your life—traveling the world, buying a home, getting married, having children, sending them to college, and, finally, retiring. It's a career arc that you are just starting, and many of the millennial generation are frustrated that they haven't started on that arc where they'd like.

Chapter 5 explores how to land a job, negotiate the first salary, and find your place in the workforce. *This* chapter lays out the fundamentals of what is a healing labor market.

One of my favorite parts of this job is covering breaking employment figures every month on CNN's morning show *New Day*. On the first Friday of every month at precisely 8:30 a.m. Eastern time, the U.S. Department of Labor releases the Employment Situation Summary—dozens of pages of tables and analysis of the U.S. labor market. The numbers are critical to understanding the health of the nation's economy. A reading below expectations can move stock and bond markets. Presidents and political parties write press releases about it. Economists, recruiters, bank executives, and journalists scour it to glean information about how well the economy is recovering and where jobs are growing in America.

I like to think of all the various jobs market statistics as the dashboard of a car. The speedometer is the unemployment rate. In the aftermath of the Crash of 2008, it rose as high as 10 percent—a level not seen since the recession of the 1980s. Double-digit unemployment is profoundly dangerous for a society where work and earnings are so central to the health of the economy and the nation's psyche. People without decent-paying jobs can't live up to their potential as consumers, savers, and investors.

Another gauge in that report is the total nonfarm payroll figure. It measures net jobs gained or lost during the month. A healthy economy is creating at least 250,000 net new jobs a month. At the worst of the crisis, the economy was shedding 700,000 jobs a month. In two years after the Crash of 2008, 8.7 million jobs were wiped out.[2] It took until the beginning of 2014 to dig out of that hole.

Consider the labor force participation rate the "check engine" light on the dashboard. This is the percentage of the working-age population employed or looking for work. That number has declined steadily in the years since the crash, falling into the low 60 percent range as people simply drop out of the labor market. (See Figure 4.1.) This statistic shows an economy that is not working for everyone and a labor market that is leaving some behind.

To CNN viewers, I often describe it as an asterisk job market. For every good statistic there is another one that shows the damage done by the recession. The unemployment rate has fallen! Yes, but millions of

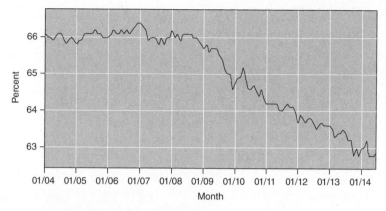

Figure 4.1   How Much of America Is Working?

Source: Bureau of Labor Statistics

Table 4.1   Jobless Rates by Educational Achievement

Educational achievement	Bachelor's degree holder	Bachelor's degree holder under age 25 (not seasonally adjusted)	High school graduate, no college	High school graduate with some college, or associate's degree
Unemployment rate	3.2%	8.2%	6.2%	5.4%

Source: Bureau of Labor Statistics, September 2014

people are working part-time and would rather be working full-time.[3] The unemployment rate for a bachelor's degree holder in September 2014 was a low 3.2 percent! Yes, but for a bachelor's degree holder under age 25, the jobless rate is more than twice that.[4] Table 4.1 shows the jobless rates by educational achievement.

THE LONG HEALING PROCESS

The Crash of 2008 was so deep and devastating, it is taking years to overcome it. Ancient history? Not really. It doesn't matter whether you were in eighth grade when the economy cratered or you were just entering college then, the echo of that collapse is still felt today. And this is why the best minds in business and economics still argue about how well the U.S. labor market is recovering—and what we *should* be doing to help it.

Mohamed El-Erian, a legendary investor and chief economic adviser for Allianz, describes the job market to me this way: He says it is "turning."

"We're creating a lot of jobs again and long-term unemployment, while still too high, is coming down and teenage unemployment is coming down," El-Erian told me. Here's the asterisk again: Wages are not rising, and he's concerned about that labor force participation rate, nearly the lowest since 1978. It's a concern shared by Carly Fiorina, former CEO of Hewlett-Packard and a Republican presidential adviser, who worries the recovery is leaving a lot of people behind.

"You have a middle class that continues to be hollowed out. You have more small businesses failing and fewer starting than in any time in 40 years . . . . In other words, there are still real problems in this economy," she told me.

One drag on the economy has been the lack of spending by corporate America on everything from new computers to tools, buildings, and people. The financial crisis caused even healthy companies to struggle to meet financial obligations, and it shattered the confidence of executives running businesses big and small, forcing them to pull back severely on spending plans. Companies from Apple to engine maker Eaton have record amounts of cash just sitting in the bank. Apple alone has more cash and international reserves than not only Microsoft and GE, but entire countries like Poland, South Africa, Turkey, and Israel.[5] Harvard professor and financial crisis expert Ken Rogoff notes that this is one reason this financial rebound is taking time.

"We got hit by a monster financial crisis, worst since the Great Depression," he told me. "You know it's getting better, but there is a long healing process."

FASTEST-GROWING STATES

The irony is that, as painful as this recovery has been for many, stocks have continued to climb, leaving most everyone who has a 401(k) or some money in the market feeling like their wallet is bigger. A recovering housing market and soaring values for energy and tech businesses and the property surrounding them in places like California, Washington, North Dakota, and Oklahoma are only boosting economic morale, not to mention economic growth. Energy, in fact, was the key driver in 6 out of the 10 fastest-growing states in 2013.[6]

The U.S. economy grew only 1.8 percent in 2013, but these 10 states outpaced the nation:

1. North Dakota
2. Wyoming
3. West Virginia
4. Oklahoma
5. Idaho
6. Colorado
7. Utah
8. Texas
9. South Dakota
10. Nebraska

This is more evidence of why many investors, including Wilbur Ross, one of the top turnaround financiers in the world, are bullish about the rebounding U.S. economy and have already made a killing on it. The theory goes that the new technology around extracting fossil fuels like oil and natural gas from the ground is changing the United States from a net importer of oil to a potential exporter. And with this new demand for U.S. oil and gas from around the world comes demand for new and improved roads and bridges, rail lines, gas pipelines, even retail, restaurants, hotels and housing to service and shelter the new employees streaming into states such as North Dakota, Pennsylvania, and Texas.

It's already happening, and you should expect that to be one of the biggest, if not *the* biggest, drivers of our economy in the coming years.

Another driver that will have a huge impact on millennials is retiring baby boomers. They've already started, but the pace will pick up in the coming years and hit some sectors more than others, according to a report by The Conference Board.[7] Among the sectors hardest hit by boomer retirements (aka the biggest job opportunities for millennials):

- *Health-related occupations.* The same aging of the U.S. population that will curtail working-age population growth to as low as 0.15 percent by 2030 is also driving up demand for medical workers. At the same time, high education and experience requirements limit entry into the job market. The result is a dearth in many health care professions, including occupational therapy assistants, physical therapists and therapist assistants, nurse practitioners and midwives, and dental hygienists. Among doctors, optometrists and podiatrists are the specialists most at risk of shortage, with the general physicians and surgeons categories not far behind.

- *Skilled labor occupations.* These jobs typically require more than a high school education, but not a bachelor's degree. Unlike in health care, the primary driver of shortages here is not increased demand—employment growth is expected to be low in the coming decade—but, instead, a rapidly shrinking supply of young people entering these fields as increasing numbers retire. Skilled labor occupations most at risk include water and wastewater treatment plant and system operators, crane and tower operators, transportation inspectors, and construction and building inspectors.

- *STEM occupations.* U.S. policy makers have long been concerned about shortages in science, technology, engineering, and mathematics, but many of these fields rank surprisingly average in a national context. Moderating the risk of shortages is the relatively high number of young entrants compared to baby boomer retirees, as well as the large proportion of new immigrants in STEM jobs. Moreover, strong productivity growth means that output will continue to expand in areas like information technology, telecommunications, and high-tech manufacturing even as workforces in these jobs are expected to shrink. Nevertheless, certain STEM fields—including mathematical science, information security, and civil, environmental, biomedical, and agricultural engineering—do face significant shortages.

Source: The Conference Board

THE COLLEGE DEGREE ADVANTAGE

25%

ROMANS'
NUMERAL

Share of bachelor's degree earners who gain little economic benefit from the degree.[8]

Here's some shocking analysis from Jaison Abel and Richard Deitz at the New York Federal Reserve. They concluded that the economic benefits of college far outweigh the costs,[9] and that average wages for college graduates are significantly higher than the same wages for those with only a high school degree. But here's the terrifying part: The Fed economists boiled the numbers down further and plotted the median annual wages for the twenty-fifth percentile of college graduates, which are the lowest earners with a college degree.

The results are stunning. Comparing the median annual earnings of a bachelor's degree holder, a high school graduate, and the bottom quarter of bachelor's degree wage earners, the Fed researchers found that "a good number of college graduates earn wages that are not materially different from those of the typical worker with just a high school diploma."

If you believe the Fed study, it means that a quarter of college graduates will face no better prospects than a high school graduate. The researchers conclude: "This suggests that at least from an economic perspective, college may not pay off for a significant number of people."

The top line on the chart in Figure 4.2 is the proof that college is worth it, and most college graduates have great days ahead in the U.S. labor market. The bottom two lines on that chart show that statistically college is worth it overall, but not for everyone.

COLLEGE MAY NOT PAY OFF FOR EVERYONE

"Overall, these figures suggest that perhaps a quarter of those who earn a bachelor's degree pay the costs to attend school but reap little, if any, economic benefit. In fact, once the costs of attending college are considered, it is likely that earning a bachelor's degree would not have been a good investment for many in the lowest 25 percent of college graduate wage earners. So while a college degree appears to be a good investment on average, it may not pay off for everyone."

—*Jaison Abel and Richard Deitz*

Reports like this are troubling but only reinforce my analysis that college is worth it, with caveats. You can't take longer than four years to graduate, you can't drop out, and you can't borrow a ton of money if you are entering

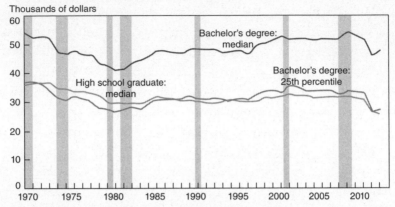

Annual Wage by Education, 1970–2013

Notes: Dollar figures are expressed in constant 2013 dollars. Shaded areas indicate periods designated recessions by the National Bureau of Economic Research.

Figure 4.2   Beware of the Bottom 25 Percent
Source: U.S. Census Bureau and U.S. Bureau of Labor Statistics, Current Population Survey, March Supplement; U.S. Bureau of Labor Statistics, consumer price index

a low-pay career field. The Fed study shows that for a huge chunk of millennials at work, their pay is not getting a boost from the investment in a bachelor's degree. Why? As you can see in Figure 4.2, the lowest quarter of bachelor's degree holders have historically more closely tracked the earnings of high school graduates. This is not a recent trend. It may be that these workers are *choosing* to work in lower-paid fields. It could be that a significant portion of high school graduates have skills and street smarts that allow them to compete with a quarter of college grads. It could be that colleges are accepting and graduating a lot of American kids who are just … *below average.*

Below average is a dangerous place to be in today's labor market. The largest, fastest-growing parts of the jobs market often require few skills and have scant benefits. Home health care, restaurants, fast food, bartending, hotels, cleaning services—executives in all these fields tell me they are desperate for workers. Turnover is high, but the pay remains low. A degree is not necessary for these fields (although training and certification are required for home health aides), and everyone has heard and read the horror stories about overeducated millennials working these jobs, biding their time for the labor market to improve enough to get better-paying jobs in their fields of study.

This low-wage job explosion has spawned a national movement to raise the pay of these jobs. Twenty-six states and the District of Columbia have already raised the minimum wage from the federal level of $7.25 an hour. In Seattle, the minimum wage is $15 an hour. Fast-food workers in 150 cities have staged protests and rallies for better pay and the right to form unions. Forty hours of full-time work a week at the typical fast-food wage of $9 an hour yields only $18,500 a year in earnings. The national conversation over the value of a person's work is only getting started.

At the other end of the spectrum—STEM (Science, Technology, Engineering, and Math, as covered in Chapter 2), Silicon Valley, and skilled manufacturing—talent is rewarded. There are hiring wars for workers with the right skills or education. Once hired, there are ample benefits, top salaries, and bonuses. In these areas, millennials are changing the way we think about the office and the ways in which we work.

Chapter 4 Action Plan

There are millions of job openings in the United States, but the trick is positioning yourself in the part of the labor market that has higher pay and better security AND keeps you challenged and happy. The job market is healing and rewarding college graduates in Science, Technology, Engineering, and Math (STEM), in economics, and in fast-growing health care. The greatest number of jobs is being created in low-wage industries. If you're biding time in a low-wage job, look for opportunities that are "ladder" jobs—providing extra training and a chance to become a manager. Where you live is key: The oil industry is booming, providing huge job growth in states such as North Dakota and Texas. And remember, the U.S. job market is the most dynamic in the world. After the recession of the early 1990s, young workers felt underemployed and frustrated in jobs like bartending. In the decade after, 24 million new jobs were created and companies were scrambling to find workers.

CHAPTER 5

Millennials at Work

ROMANS'
NUMERAL

50%

Millennials will make up half of the U.S. workforce by 2020.

Let's get this out of the way right away. Millennials have a pretty bad reputation in the workplace. Don't shoot the messenger—I'm not saying the stereotypes (Google the phrase "millennials at work" and you'll find insults) are correct, but you'll have to be careful to prove them wrong on your own. In any job interview or corporate setting, it pays to be aware that somewhere in the back of the mind of the hiring manager, there is fear that you have an unrealistically high opinion of yourself and that your parents never made you work hard for anything.

Millennials will be about half the workforce in the next few years, so hiring, training, and promoting good millennial talent is critical for companies. But human resources departments are struggling with how to manage millennials. Sean Bisceglia of Scout Exchange, an electronic recruitment marketplace, surveyed 20,000 human resources managers and found plenty of troubling stereotypes.

The people who hire and manage millennials say they're pretty worried about some of your generation's work habits. Most don't want to work more than 40 hours a week, and many lack person-to-person skills.

"Young employees have overoptimistic expectations about how quickly they'll climb up the corporate ladder," Bisceglia wrote in an opinion piece in the *Chicago Tribune*.[1]

Hiring bosses noted a "frustrating" sense of entitlement. According to Bisceglia's survey: "As one HR professional noted, the younger employees felt they are owed more respect, opportunity and pay than their experience, ability or knowledge merit."

Your goals and expectations will help change the job market. I fully expect the job market you enter today to be unrecognizable by the time you retire. Some of the brightest minds in the world are looking for ways to disrupt the nine-to-five workplace and think differently about work and our place in it.

Google cofounder Larry Page sees a future with a four-day workweek and more free time for people to create, invent, and enjoy life. The Google pursuit of self-driving cars, the theory goes, will cut commute times and lead to more green space and less space devoted to parking. Amazon wants drones to drop your purchases at your front door, saving you valuable time for other pursuits.

How would you like a four-day weekend – every week?! Carlos Slim, the Mexican media tycoon worth more than $80 billion, told me he thinks a three-day workweek is inevitable.

"You should have more time for you during all of your life—not when you are 65 and retired." If Slim had his way, people would work longer days and for longer in their life, but enjoy 4-day weekends throughout. Younger workers and radical new technologies will revolutionaize economies and financial markets.

We asked New Yorkers what they thought about Slim's advice. I'd say the reaction was mixed. The video is here:

http://www.cnn.com/video/data/2.0/video/living/2014/07/21/orig-jag -3-day-work-week.cnn.html

On the other end of the spectrum are the hackathons at Facebook, where engineers work all night to finish projects. At many tech firms, employees are encouraged to take 20 percent of their work time to pursue pet projects. The idea is innovation, not punching a clock.

Tech is the ultimate millennial-friendly job landscape. But it is predominantly male, and a relatively narrow set of skills is required. It's ironic that the author of the seminal book on women at work, Sheryl Sandberg and *Lean In,* works for a company where 69 percent of its global staffers are male and 77 percent of its management team are men.[2]

Facebook acknowledges it has work to do in the diversity department, and its numbers are reflective of the "brogrammer" culture of Silicon Valley.

What's interesting here is that as much as Silicon Valley exists to thwart the exclusive, power-suit culture of Wall Street (Mark Zuckerberg wearing a hoodie to meet investors in New York as the company was about to go public is a prime example), it's still very similar. Like bankers on Wall Street, it does take an "eat what you kill" mentality to really be successful in Silicon Valley. That type of person is still greatly prized.

I report about the two-speed jobs recovery. In one jobs market, there is a low-wage jobs explosion and double-digit underemployment. In the other, there are wars for talent and companies are opening their wallets to keep good people happy.

Data from human resources giant Aon Hewitt show that these superstars on the job are being rewarded. As the job market improves, top companies have to compete to keep their best workers, and that has led more companies to offer performance-related bonuses. In 2014, companies paid out record employee bonuses[3] and were forecast to do even better in 2015. While the pace of salary increases is modest, Aon found more companies were keeping their workers happy with bonuses instead. Back in 2005, only 78 percent of companies offered performance bonuses. In 2014, that number was 91 percent. Where the typical salaried employee might see a 10 to 20 percent bonus, the superstars are seeing 15 to 40 percent bumps.

Raises are also higher for the best of the best, but performance isn't the only factor. Location and industry play big roles. Aon Hewitt found the best raises in Denver, Houston, and Los Angeles—all higher than 3.2 percent. In New York, Minneapolis–St. Paul, and Milwaukee, raises are somewhat less—around 2.8 percent or lower. Table 5.1 shows that some industries have better salary increases than others. Why does it matter? If your raise is 3 percent and the consumer inflation rate is 3 percent, then you really don't get much of a raise at all.

In Silicon Valley, the quest for talent is relentless. Top companies like Facebook and Yahoo! have perfected what is known as the *acqui-hire*.

Table 5.1   Employee Pay Raises, 2015

Industry	Average annual bonus (%)
Gas and oil	3.8
Education	2.7
Government	2.6
Paper products	2.6
Overall	3.0

Source: Aon Hewitt

Mark Zuckerberg and Marissa Mayer will acquire start-ups and established companies alike just so they can bring their talented engineers on board.

Silicon Valley has replaced Wall Street as a top draw for many über-educated math whizzes, economists, and finance majors. The lifestyle, the perks, the ethos, and, frankly, the millennial focus of tech land have some Wall Street titans quietly changing how they compensate top young talent.

According to *CNNMoney*, banks are scrambling to boost their pay packages for the young best of the best. Goldman Sachs, JPMorgan Chase, and Bank of America are expected to raise some junior-level salaries by about 20 percent, *CNNMoney*'s sources say.[4]

That would bring an entry-level analyst at Goldman Sachs (the bottom step of the investment banking ladder) about $85,000 a year in salary. The pay hikes are meant to keep rivals from poaching top talent and keep top talent from being lured away by Google, Microsoft, Yahoo!, Facebook, and any of a number of venture capital and tech investing companies. At the same time, other banks are doing away with some of the most hated aspects of the legendary punishing schedules of young people in finance.

"The number one reason why young people leave finance is the lifestyle: working 100-hour weeks and being on call constantly," Scott Rostan, a former banker at Merrill Lynch who now runs a Wall Street business education firm, tells *CNNMoney*. "That's brutal and very, very difficult to keep up with in the long term."

In a private conversation, one top bank CEO acknowledged to me that millennials are driven differently than previous generations, who hungrily wanted to climb straight up the ladder, working 18-hour days to do it. Millennials are watching their friends start companies in dorm rooms, or dropping out and working for tech start-ups, and realizing there are other avenues to success.

In the end, he said, millennials are just as ambitious. They want to succeed, but they want to do it on their own terms.

Really, the tech revolution of the past 15 years or so has defined your generation, and your generation is defining a culture shift in how we work.

Motorola is a great example. It's a storied technology company that for years was based in Schaumburg, Illinois—a sleepy Chicago suburb with big houses and golf courses, where a car is requisite for getting anywhere. Today Motorola occupies the Merchandise Mart in downtown Chicago, with state-of-the-art labs and design studios. It is here, in a landmark Chicago building with free lunchrooms and funky dens, that some of the most exciting developments in battery size and life, cell technology, voice recognition technology, and wearables are taking place. To attract the best designers and engineers and to compete with Silicon Valley in California and Silicon Alley in New York, Motorola rebooted its workspace.

The Silicon Valley ethos is spreading to Chicago, Pittsburgh, and New York—the tech presence is not just on the West Coast anymore.

In fact, plenty of graduates with four-year degrees are jumping into intensive coding programs to add another level to their education. In New York, DevbootCamp is a 19-week course, for about $12,000, that teaches students web development and coding. After "graduation" job placement is near 100 percent. It's one of several programs like it around the country tapping into the need for technical skills on top of a traditional college education. To see my CNN profile of DevBootCamp:

http://www.cnn.com/video/data/2.0/video/cnnmoney/2014/11/14
/ivory-coding.cnnmoney.html

34%

A third of the jobs in America are held by freelancers.[5]

For evidence that the workforce is more flexible and self-directed, look no further than the army of freelancers doing so much of the nation's work.

Table 5.2   Freelancing and Millennials

	Under 35 years old	Over 35 years old
Freelancing	38%	32%
Optimistic about the future of the freelance job market	82%	74%

Source: "Freelancing in America: A National Survey of the New Workforce," Edelman Berland for Freelancers Union and Elance-oDesk

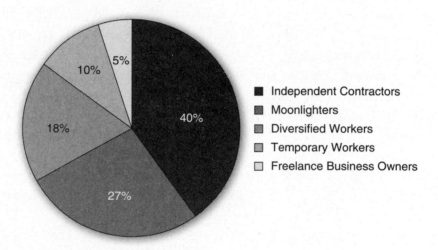

Figure 5.1   Five Freelancer Segments
Source: "Freelancing in America: A National Survey of the New Workforce," Edelman Berland for Freelancers Union and Elance-oDesk

Millennials are more likely to freelance than any other generation, and they are the most optimistic about it (see Table 5.2).

"Freelancing is the new normal," says Sara Horowitz, founder and executive director of Freelancers Union. She calls the freelance workforce "big, crucial, and here to stay." Technology allows young workers to more easily find freelance work, collaborate with clients, and get paid on time—the three traditional barriers for freelancers (see Figure 5.1).

RESUME #FAIL

I often advise young people to "mind the gap" on their resume and make sure that any gaps in meaningful work experience are filled with other professional-looking endeavors. For example, let's say you had a short unpaid internship the summer after graduation but no "real" job after that. While sending out resumes and looking for work, you handled your uncle's pizza place's social media profile in exchange for free food. My advice would be to play up the social media business on the resume and give some great examples of how you added customers or modernized his profile.

What I never recommend is lying.

An astonishing 58 percent of employers say they have caught a lie on a resume, according to a Harris poll conducted for CareerBuilder.[6]

"Trust is very important in professional relationships, and by lying on your resume, you breach that trust from the very outset," said Rosemary Haefner, vice president of human resources at CareerBuilder. "If you want to enhance your resume, it's better to focus on playing up the tangible examples from your actual experience."

Most Common Resume Lies

- Embellished skill set 57%
- Embellished responsibilities 55%
- Dates of employment 42%
- Job title 34%
- Academic degrees 33%
- Companies worked for 26%
- Accolades/awards 18%

CareerBuilder's survey asked employers to describe the most memorable lies they had spotted on resumes. Some are stunning in their audacity, and others are so lame it is painful. One job seeker claimed to be his father (with the same name) and put his father's experience and work history on the resume. Another applicant claimed to have been a "construction supervisor." Later in the hiring process, the interviewer discovered the bulk of this candidate's experience consisted of building a doghouse some years before. Another candidate applied twice for the same position and provided a different work history for each application. Yet another claimed to be an assistant to the prime minister of a country that does not have a prime minister. Your resume should be relevant for the company and position you are seeking, and, above all, it should be true.

What might seem like a little white lie when you are getting started in your career can be devastating down the road—and by devastating I mean it can cost you your job. Some high-profile fibs that cost jobs include one told by Yahoo! CEO Scott Thompson, who claimed he had a degree in computer science (he didn't), and RadioShack CEO David Edmondson, who resigned when it was reported that he did not have the two college degrees he included on his resume. And it's not just in corporate America, either. Remember Federal Emergency Management Agency (FEMA) director Michael Brown of "Brownie, you're doing a heck of a job," fame during George W. Bush's administration? It wasn't mishandling Hurricane Katrina relief that cost him his job. It was his claims that he ran the emergency services unit for Edmund, Oklahoma, when in fact he was more of an intern as the assistant to the city. And, of course, there is the notorious five-day stint for George O'Leary as head coach of the Notre Dame football team, arguably the pinnacle of college coaching. He lost his job after it was discovered he did not get a master's degree in education from New York University and never played in a game for the University of New Hampshire, both which were on his resume.

Unfortunately, I could go on, but I think by now you get the point: Any lies or embellishments on your resume now will eventually derail the great accomplishments you are going for. It's never worth it.

YOU'VE GOT TWO MINUTES

The typical hiring manager will spend about two minutes reviewing each resume, CareerBuilder estimates. Most employers (86 percent) typically have more than one employee review candidates' resumes. Your resume and cover letter need to be relevant, accurate, and powerful. Your cover letter has to hook the reader in the first sentence. After that, it needs a fast-paced and exciting narrative to pull the interviewer in. If you are like most of us, you will find yourself writing a two-page cover letter. Cut it in half, and then trim it some more. Keep it tight. Here's why: When Brad Karsh, author of *How to Say It on Your Resume* (Prentice Hall, 2009) and a frequent guest on CNN, was a recruiting director, he received 10,000 resumes and 9,000 cover letters. He says applicants should expect a hiring manager or recruiter to spend 10 seconds scanning the cover letter and another 10 seconds on the resume. (See samples of good and bad cover letters in Appendix B of this book.)

Those 10 seconds turn into a full read only if there is a narrative hook, no mistakes, and a clear idea that the applicant is showing that his or her skills fit the company.

Most people just rewrite their resumes into a cover letter. Instead, Karsh says, "you have to think of the cover letter as a movie trailer." He says most job applicants include the same four boring paragraphs: how you heard about the job, why you are interested, why you'd be great at it, and, finally, how you are going to follow up. "You've written a lot of words and essentially given me no information," says Karsh.

Avoid empty buzzwords like *facilitate, transition,* and *utilize,* and instead make sure you understand the lingo of the industry you are seeking a job in. Merely using fancy words that you think sound like they should be from business school will not impress a hiring manager.

Just say what you mean in simple, clear language. (And everyone says they are a team player and a problem solver. Those go without saying.)

Managers are busy people, with lots of office problems to solve. "Don't waste my time if you aren't going to add value," Karsh says.

So go into it knowing that your competitors for that job will have similar if not better education and work experience. What makes *you* stand out from the rest? Why would the hiring manager plug you into his or her team? What makes you good in the trenches with your future teammates? These details and anecdotes can oftentimes be the hook that you need to get your foot in the door.

THE HIDDEN JOBS MARKET

You'll have the greatest success if you know of a specific person to send your cover letter and resume to. Ideally, you will be sending your cover letter and resume to someone who knows they are coming. You've heard it from everyone from counselors and the university career office to colleagues at the office: *Network!*

Network is both a noun and a verb and it is the most overused word in the jobs market. The trouble for young workers is that you are just getting started, so your network isn't yet chock-full of people who know you and can vouch for your work.

Ellen Gordon Reeves is a career adviser and author of *Can I Wear My Nose Ring to the Interview?* (Workman, 2009). She has a simple mantra: "Stop looking for a job and start looking for a person. The right person will lead you to the right job."

She says the most important line on the cover letter is the one that contains the name of the person referring you—the common connection between you and the person reading the letter. For example:

> Dear Mr. Buffett, Christine Romans recommended that I speak with you.

Make a personal connection that ensures the reader spends more than the typical 10 seconds and instead devotes two full minutes to reviewing your material.

"Concentrate on lining up as many information interviews as you can," Reeves says. "You've got to get yourself and your resume in front of as many people as possible. Stop wasting your own time by sending your resume hurtling into the black void of cyberspace."

Many, if not most, jobs are never posted or advertised. Reeves calls this the hidden jobs market. By some estimates it constitutes as much as 80 percent of the jobs market. A hiring manager gets a personal referral and, rather than post the position, fills it with someone who knows someone. It's a much better scenario for the harried hiring manager—trusting the reference from a common acquaintance or employee, rather than picking through thousands of bloated resumes that, frankly, all say the same thing.

For many tech companies, much of the hiring takes place through word of mouth. Employees at the top tech companies get referral bonuses for finding great hires for the company, so it pays to keep your connections fresh.

One of the best anecdotes that I know of about networking at a young age comes from a good friend who works at one of the titans of Silicon Valley. He referred a young college grad to his old job in sales when it came up, even though this candidate had no tech experience and lived thousands of miles from California. But the referral got him an interview. This college grad was gregarious and enthusiastic and showed incredible salesmanship.

The first thing the hiring manager said after the interview: "I have no idea if he knows anything about technology, but I'd buy a thousand pounds of pasta from him right now!" Impressions count. Interview skills are critical to make connections with bosses across the table from you. The "pasta salesman" got the job and is traveling the country selling advertising on a major search engine.

That says it all. A network can get you in the door and allow you to win over the people trying to fill the job, no matter how much experience you have. So throw out the "I don't have experience" attitude. Of course you do. Every internship, senior project, part-time job, professional association, or volunteer job helps paint a picture of what kind of employee you will be.

There are so many smart ways to create the connections and experiences you can use later for your resume. Internships are the most obvious—and the most critical. They allow you to meet people in the workforce who can be references for you later and who can give you a heads-up when a real job for which you are suited arises. Often, the best internships are competitive and sometimes unpaid—a problem for many students. (My parents, by the way, would not let me take unpaid internships. For them, it was an affront that an hour of my labor would not be compensated, and I wholeheartedly agree. This forced me to work harder to find jobs—and I certainly needed the money.) The best candidates for jobs are coming from college with multiple internships, so even nabbing something for the summer after graduation is a great idea.

Consider a "job shadow." Tap the alumni network from your college or degree program for mentors who will let you spend one day or a week shadowing them at work. Tap old neighbors, friends, or relatives—anyone you may have a connection with who is doing something that interests you. More times than not this person will remember what it's like and take you on board or help connect you. You'll meet people—be friendly, get business cards and contacts, and connect with people on LinkedIn. All of this is a potential foot in the door later on.

Speaking of LinkedIn, social media is a big help—and a potential minefield—for you. Obviously, you are smart enough not to have a public Facebook or Twitter feed full of party pictures or political rants. (Right?!)

Here's an anecdote to consider: I was moderating a panel of commercial real estate CEOs in front of students at Florida State University, and I asked one of the CEOs his best advice for job seekers. His response caused 150 students to gasp.

He said he had revoked a six-figure job offer to a job candidate who had looked great on paper, with impeccable grades, a top internship, and great references from professors. He revoked the job offer because the candidate was sloppy and drunk on Facebook and incredibly immature and opinionated in postings on other social media.

"He did not seem like a serious enough or thoughtful enough person for a job of this level of income and responsibility," he said.

"Google yourself. And look at your Facebook page as if you are the boss," he recommended. His exasperation—and the students' shock—has stuck with me. It shows a huge disconnect between those who want to get hired and those doing the hiring. Would a fellow millennial CEO take a more forgiving view? Possibly. But it is not worth the risk—you want a job.

Another executive in hotel and restaurant management told me the final screening he does when promoting someone to a management position in his resorts and hotels is a close look at the candidate's online presence. Too much partying is a big red flag, as are overt political affiliations. In the hospitality business, you need to be hospitable to everyone. Discretion is a virtue.

Yes, you have a right to privacy. Yes, you can keep personal content private. But you should be prepared for a human resources manager to "friend" you during the hiring process.

So Google yourself. Clean up the old Facebook page. Use Snapchat and Cyber Dust for anything NSFW (not safe for work).

DON'T CALL THEM SOFT SKILLS

Integrity and professionalism are the top qualities that employers value, surveys show.

These used to be called "soft skills," but workplace experts and human resources managers say there is nothing soft about them at all. The hard truth is that companies need talent that can collaborate and lead. These skills are critical, and you can't get a degree in them.

In fact, when asked to rank eight top qualities of job applicants, education ranked dead last, in a survey from Express Employment Professionals, a staffing firm based in Oklahoma City, with 700 franchises in the United States, Canada, and South Africa.[7] Here is the complete list:

1. Attitude
2. Work ethic/integrity
3. Credible work history
4. Culture fit
5. Specific skills
6. Job experience
7. References
8. Education

"Even the best education is no substitute for a good attitude," says CEO Bob Funk. "Of course education is important, but while employers can teach their employees new skills, it's much more difficult to teach things like integrity, work ethic, or attitude."

His advice for job seekers: "You're much more than your resume. Employers don't just want someone who has the skills and knowledge to succeed. They are looking for people they can work with on a daily basis and trust to represent their companies well," Funk says. Leadership skills and attitude are two qualities that are so difficult to assess through a resume or cover letter, and they are another reason why a common connection and personal references are so important. Think of it this way: These attributes can easily set *you* apart from the millions of bright, driven, hungry college grads entering the workforce every year. What is it about you that can help the hiring manager's business succeed? Be prepared to sell them on that in the interview.

Bosses often tell me that they hire a worker because they have a problem to solve and they need to find the right person with the right skills to solve it. Do your best to identify the company's problem and convince the hiring manager you can solve it. And don't be intimidated by the competition out there. The fancy school on the resume will never beat out polished communication skills, hard work, and likability. Ken Langone, the billionaire cofounder of Home Depot, says it best: "The world is run by C students."

KEEP YOUR EYE ON THE BALL

Those C students can often become top performers at a job because they have the mix of skills, attitude, and drive to get the job done. But don't fall into one of the biggest traps employees face when they start to lose interest in their current job and want to try something else: Their performance falls off in the job they are doing right now. Say you've been in a job for a few years and are applying for another position, either within or outside your current employer. Who is the hiring manager for the new position you seek going to turn to for information about your work, attitude, and so forth? Look no further than your current boss and colleagues. If you have been slacking off and not meeting the expectations of your boss and colleagues in your current role, why on earth would someone want to bring you onto their team? This is really important if you are looking to move within the company you work for now. But even if you want out and move to another company or institution, don't fool yourself—it *is* a small world after all. As *big* as they may seem, most industries are tight-knit when it comes to personnel—especially high performers worth poaching. If you've been in the workforce for more than a few years, people know you, and if they don't, it doesn't take long to find people who do.

This type of situation speaks to the professionalism we covered earlier in this chapter. You see it happen time and time again at work: People lose interest, or they don't get along with others on their team and their motivation falters. Oftentimes, they don't realize they are falling into that trap. But you have to fight through it and be a pro—don't let small things impact your performance. More times than not, it costs people the new job they so covet because they are taking their eye off the ball in the job they have.

LEAN IN OR LEAN BACK

It's safe to say Sheryl Sandberg is not a C student. And, yes, she does run the world (or, at least, Facebook). She's the company's chief operating officer and the author of *Lean In,* a book that started a frank discussion about how women should lean into their careers and value themselves. Sandberg says now is the time for women to double down on their careers, with no apologies, to take their places in decision-making and leadership roles, and not to underestimate what they can accomplish at work.

"Women are getting more college degrees, more graduate degrees and entering the workforce at every level," Sandberg says. "But in industry after industry, women are at 18, 15, 20 percent of the top jobs."[8] Among Fortune 500 companies, there are just 26 chief executive officers who are women. (An all-time high, yes, but it's still just 5.2 percent.)[9]

"I think the world would be a better place if half the countries and companies were run by women and half the homes were run by men," Sandberg says.[10] Men dominate the leadership roles in the United States, and they make more money—whether they are janitors or teachers or engineers or bankers. Until there is equality in leadership, there will continue to be distinct inequality in what women earn. In virtually every job category women earn less for the same hour of work than men do—about 82 cents on the dollar. It is not that women work less or are in lower-paying positions. Even when adjusting for industry, women make less than what men are making in 101 of 112 occupations.[11]

There is now—for the first time in my lifetime—a national conversation about gender bias in the workplace and how women can "lean in" to achieve more. The good news is that women today have the option to pursue their careers with abandon and work to whittle those wage differences.

Economists have long argued about why women make less. There is a complicated mix of reasons.

There's just plain old discrimination. And there is timing. Many hit the sweet spot of their career just as they reach the peak of their family building. That means taking an off-ramp for a few months—or even longer—to have a baby. Some relocate for their husband's job. Women are still more likely to work *and* manage the household (arranging for day care or a nanny, cleaning, paying bills), though men are rapidly making up ground here.

At work, men are more likely to ask for a raise or negotiate it more forcefully. I've heard behavioral economists theorize that because men have played sports from a young age, they know how to work within a team and at the same time be aggressive about getting what *they* want. (The good news here is that is changing; more girls are playing a wider variety of sports than ever before.)

One reason could be as simple as the fact that women are more likely to accept the first salary they are offered and men are more likely to respond to a job offer with a higher counteroffer.

A bit here on women and negotiating. Columbia University professor Lee Miller, who, with his daughter Jessica Miller, wrote the book *A Woman's Guide to Successful Negotiating* (McGraw-Hill, 2010), believes a reluctance to haggle over salary holds too many women back.

Consider this: Lee says a $5,000 raise at age 22 is equal to about a half million dollars in salary and benefits over the course of a lifetime.[12]

"Women tend to ask for less," says Miller, who teaches classes on negotiating at Columbia University. "And the corollary to that is you are going to get less."

But Miller points out something amazing. Young, single, childless women living in metropolitan areas are outearning men their age.[13] It's more evidence that the millennial generation could well change many of the trends that have marked the labor market since women first started going to work in the middle of the previous century. What happens when those women start raising families? We can only hope the pay gap doesn't reemerge.

Whatever the reasons, there are still big divides between men and women in the workplace. Maybe it is a sign of progress that whether to "lean in" isn't the only conversation men and women are having about life and work. For the first time ever, we're asking for more out of our careers than just climbing a ladder and getting a big paycheck.

It's fair to say that Arianna Huffington is a workaholic rewarded with great success for believing in a good idea, taking risks, and working hard. She is the editor in chief of the wildly successful *Huffington Post* and author of *Thrive* (Harmony, 2014).

She tells a chilling story about collapsing from exhaustion in her office in 2007, breaking her cheekbone and hurting her eye. It was then that she realized success came at a very big price. "That's what started me asking these big questions like, what is a good life, what is success?" she says. If "the definition of success was lying on the floor of my office in a pool of blood, I was not successful."

"The two metrics of success, money and power, are not really a complete life," Huffington told me. "And, it's like trying to sit on a two-legged stool. So the third metric of success, for me, consists of these four pillars: well-being or health first; wisdom, a capacity to be able to connect with our own wisdom and intuition; wonder, not to miss life, not to miss the delight and joy of life; and giving, giving has to be a big component of life."

When she told me this, I was blown away. These are the things I hear young people say they want out of their careers and lives. What critics call "entitled" or "lazy," Arianna Huffington calls a need to thrive. I think it is no surprise she is the mother of millennial daughters.

She and Sandberg are friends, and their taglines—"Lean In" and "Thrive"—are not contradictory. I often ask successful women this question: "Do you lean into your job? Or do you lean back and search for balance?"

The best answer comes from fashion designer, author, and mother of two Cynthia Rowley. In her studio and showroom in New York's West Village, surrounded by clothes and accessories (and even Band-Aids) that bear her name, she surprised me. "Lean in? Or lean back?!" Rowley says and then laughs. "Are those my only choices? I just jump with a bungee cord."

How has she kept her brand fresh and her business focused over two decades in the fickle fashion world? "I love to work. I love to work. I love to work."

Whether tending bar while going to the Art Institute in Chicago, crafting product lines for Target, or participating in Fashion Week, she's driven by curiosity and has fun working.

Rowley is a third kind of example of a successful woman at work: She jumps with both feet metaphorically attached to a bungee cord and isn't afraid of the ground below or the force of the snapback.

She is incredibly optimistic about young women and men just starting out today. Worried about a slow economy for millennials? Afraid to take a risk? Disappointed that the dream job isn't there?

"I think this is a great time to start something for yourself, I really do. I mean, it has never been easier or more fun to start something, create an idea or a product and get it out to the world," Rowley says.

Time calls the Sandberg "Lean In" revolution "the most ambitious mission to re-boot feminism and reframe discussions of gender since the launch of

Ms. magazine in 1971."[14] I tend to agree. Our mother's generation was the stay-at-home-mom generation, when brave and educated women were just beginning to gain currency at work.

For gen-X women like me, Sandberg's experiences resonate. We all graduated from college and bought an "interview suit" from Ann Taylor in either black, gray, or navy. Silk blouse. Long sleeves. Basically, it was the slightly more feminine version of the suit all the men were wearing. The goal was to try to remind anyone you weren't different from men. The first wave of women who became leaders in many industries were those who emulated the way men worked. Eighteen-hour days. Golf games. Take-no-prisoners, eat-breathe-live the job.

Today, women are showing their individuality (though I still recommend some restraint at the first interview!). Men are now using the "Lean In" tactics to get better balance in their own lives and families. It's more evidence that millennials will operate in a workplace unlike anything we have seen before. They have the ability to set their own expectations for what they want to do at work. As long as they come up with ideas and perform, they will be able to shape how companies and workplaces operate. Now that's exciting.

I hate the phrase "work/life balance"—it is so incomplete in describing what women and men are looking for in their careers. The situation is never in balance. Sometimes work is the driver in your life, and sometimes when you hit your stride in your career, it allows you some flexibility to shift the balance to home and personal endeavors. The trouble comes when the scales only tilt toward work, work, work. Huffington notes that U.S. businesses lose $300 billion a year because of stressed employees. Huffington points to people like Mark Bertolini, the CEO of insurance company Aetna, who introduced yoga, meditation, and acupuncture to all his 49,000 employees. He brought in Duke University to study the results, and their researchers found a 70 percent reduction in health care costs and a $69-million-a-day increase in productivity.

"Nurture your human capital," Huffington told me when I interviewed her about her book, *Thrive*. "You are the most important thing you have. If you don't nurture yourself, you are not going to be as creative and productive. And increasingly, in this second machine age, when some of our jobs are done by machines, our creativity is the most important thing that we could bring to our jobs."

ONLINE TOOLS TO HELP SET YOU APART

One of the biggest complaints of employers in the United States is that workers don't have the skills they need in a rapidly changing—and STEM-focused—economy. They actually have a continuum of complaints. High school educators worry students don't have the math and reading base they need by fifth grade. Colleges worry that college-bound high school graduates aren't ready for college and career. As you learned in Chapter 2, college testing company ACT says only 26 percent of college-bound seniors meet minimum requirements in all four testing categories—science, math, English, and reading. By the time they reach college, up to 40 percent of students are taking remedial English (at college tuition prices) to learn what they should have learned in high school.

Clearly, from college to the workforce, skills and education are top of mind. But just a degree is not going to necessarily set you apart. And it could cost a fortune to get that degree. It's a money suck from start to finish and a system ripe for disruption.

There are exciting developments in online education that could be ideal for young learners who want to get a jump on college material and young workers looking to make their cover letter or resume shine. Called *massive open online* courses (MOOCs), these online resources provide access to elite university classes for free.

To view my story about MOOCs and their role in higher education:
http://www.cnn.com/video/?/video/cnnmoney/2014/11/14/ivory
-moocs.cnnmoney&video_referrer=http%3A%2F%2Fwww.cnn.com
%2FSPECIALS%2Fus%2Fcnn-film-ivory-tower%2Findex.html

Anant Agrawal is the CEO of edX, which offers free college—and high school AP—courses online. In 2011, he was a computer science and engineering professor at MIT, when he decided to offer his circuits and electronics course online for free. The success was instant. Now hundreds of universities and some of the most engaging and talented professors in the world are sharing their classes. You don't pay tuition, you don't get credit, but you get the education.

You want to take CS50—the same introduction to computer science class that the freshmen at Harvard take? EdX offers it for free. Want to put it on your resume? For as little as $25 you can have edX verify on your LinkedIn profile that you completed it.

After hundreds of years of delivering education in essentially the same way, online courses and technology now allow motivated learners to get access to some amazing personal development tools.

Agrawal expects big changes in how we learn and how the traditional education system responds. He's a proponent of *education bundling,* whereby high school students can use online tools to prepare for college. Then, once they are in college, they can spend two years on campus for the important experiences of collaborating with others and living away from home. Through participation in campus activities and organizations, they can also learn the soft skills and leadership ability one needs for a job. During the last college year, they can continue learning with MOOCs while being partnered with an employer and working at a job. This is an exciting prospect, and it reflects the flexibility and innovation that are trademarks of millennials.

On one thing is clear: It is critical that you have a strong base in STEM no matter what your college major and career aspirations.

"You must be STEM-literate. You absolutely must be STEM-literate," Agrawal told me. "But it's not one or the other. It has to be both liberal arts and STEM. A multidisciplinary education" produces lifelong learners who make great workers, he contends.

The liberal arts include communication skills. "You have to be able to express an idea and convince someone" to agree with your premise or project. "If you have the deep thinking and the communications skills? That combination is absolutely lethal," Agrawal says.

Chapter 5 Action Plan

College degree or not, it's time to get to work so you can start to build your wealth. Identify which skills you have that can land you a job. Be aware of the stereotypes with which some may have already labeled you before you even interview. Prove them wrong. Prioritize what is most important to you and how you define success, be it money, flexibility, long hours, travel, or big company versus start-up. Network! Keep the resume crisp and active, and don't embellish—that will come back to haunt you. Keep your cover letter tight. In the interview, do your homework on the company and on the hiring manager's background. And then expect to win them over in the interview to the point that they *want* you on their team. If you are already employed but starting to look around for something else, keep your performance level high in your existing role. When it is time to negotiate your salary, push hard for a raise. If you are that valuable, there is a market out there for your skills if your current employer is not willing to pay up.

CHAPTER

House Money

ROMANS' NUMERAL

40%

Share of the typical millennial budget going to rent or housing costs.

Let's begin with the single best personal finance move you can make today: living at home, with extended relatives or roomates. Typical millennials are spending way too much on their housing costs—on average spending 40 percent of their budget on rent, according to Level Money. For millennials who live in expensive cities like New York and Silicon Valley, the percentage can be more than half. A conservative guideline for how much of your money should be going to shelter each month is 28 percent of your pay. Some financial experts say pushing to 35 percent is reasonable in the high-cost Northeast and Silicon Valley.

You've got to get the housing costs down. Live at home, double or triple up with roommates, or live in your great-aunt's attic. Until you've got student loans under control or you've found a decent job in your major, getting a handle on housing costs is the single most critical way to live within your means.

It's smart, and it is trendy. A record 57 million Americans live in households with more than one generation, according to Pew Research. It's a return to the old days when multiple generations living under one roof made economic sense and was a social custom. My mother and grandmother each grew up with grandparents in their homes. In numerous cultures and at various socioeconomic levels, this was the norm, not the exception. Pew says the trend today is not driven by Grandma and Grandpa trying to keep their costs down during retirement by moving in with their adult children in exchange for providing child care. Especially since 2010, young Americans are coming home after college and pushing up multigenerational homeownership rates. Pew found that by 2012 roughly one in four young adults between the ages of 25 and 34 lived in a multigenerational household, more than double the rate in 1980.[1] The demographers at Pew also found that the increase in multigenerational households is seen for both genders and among most racial and ethnic groups, but Pew notes that men were slightly more likely than women to be living at home. (See Table 6.1.)

I've been bullish on multigenerational housing for several years now, first inspired by a story I reported about contractors who were specializing in renovating homes for three generations: the college graduate boomeranging back after school, the baby boomer parents, and the aging grandmother or grandfather. With rising health care and child care costs, skyrocketing rents, and huge student loans, it just makes sense.

Studies show that you millennials are in no hurry to buy houses. You're forgiven if you are scared to death of real estate. You've come of age in a terrible period during which there were more people losing their homes than becoming first-time home buyers. Foreclosures and short sales on the block where you grew up became the norm. The U.S. housing market was upside down. When millions of people live in their biggest investment and it goes belly-up, it takes time to heal.

Table 6.1   Multigenerational Living

Age	Living with multiple generations (%)
25–34	23.6
85+	22.7
Women 25–34	21
Men 25–34	26

Source: Pew Research Center Analysis of 2010–2012 American Community Survey

Make no mistake, however: The housing market has staged a stunning recovery from the bubble that burst in 2008. During the worst aftermath of the crash, median home prices were more than 30 percent below the peak reached in 2007. For millions of Americans, their most valuable asset and their biggest investment lost nearly a third of its value. For anyone who had bought real estate in the mid-2000s, it was a staggering loss. The down payment disappeared, there was no equity in the home, and if you wanted to sell you'd have to bring a big check at closing to cover the lost value of the house.

In the years since, home prices have erased the worst of those losses. After plunging to the lowest level since 1998, home prices have recovered to 2004 levels, and the distance from the peak has been whittled down to 17 percent.[2] Since March 2012, home prices have risen an astonishing 27.8 percent, and the increase is 28.5 percent for Case-Shiller's 10-City and 20-City Composite home prices indexes The housing recovery—first centered in former bubble cities such as Phoenix and Las Vegas—is broadening out. In Chicago, New York, and Detroit, home prices are recovering and foreclosures have slowed sharply. The green shoots of growth that economists look for after a crash are clearly visible in the housing market.

But those green shoots do little to erase the experience that scarred an entire generation of potential home buyers. The bubble in home prices first priced out regular homeowners—or, worse, trapped them in homes they couldn't afford. When the bust came in 2008, millions of Americans stopped paying their home loans. Across the country, foreclosure filings skyrocketed, and for the first time Americans questioned the value of homeownership.

The share of Americans who are homeowners has fallen to 64.8 percent. The homeownership rate hasn't been this low since 1995. For context, the movies *Clueless* and *Batman Forever* were in theaters then. (Yeah, since before many of you were born, basically.) Even a few years ago it would have been unheard of that so few young people were moving into residential real estate.

Instead, you are moving back home or into rentals with friends. Student debt, lower-paying jobs, or scarce jobs in your field are keeping younger people on edge about the biggest investment they will likely ever make: a home.

"I don't think millennials value home ownership like other generations," says Stephanie Genkin, the Brooklyn-based fee-only independent planner who advises millennials. "Freedom is the new American Dream for this crowd."

Most important, young people need flexibility to be able to move to a different town for a better job, or move to a new city for a job transfer or promotion.

Homeownership just doesn't have the same draw it once did.

In this new post–financial crisis world, not everyone needs to be a homeowner, and many financially savvy twenty- and thirtysomethings "don't see why they should load up on debt for the privilege of shoveling their own snow or paying someone to fix a toilet," Genkin says.

There may be little incentive to shift that dynamic for several more years, according to real estate tracker Zillow. "It could be until the end of this decade before the housing markets return to normal," Zillow chief economist Stan Humphries says. "A normal housing market is a really, really boring market."

MISSING THE REAL ESTATE REBOUND…SO FAR

There is nothing boring in the housing market right now. Rents are rising quickly. In fully a third of the country, rents are unaffordable by historic standards, according to Zillow's research. And there is certainly nothing boring about home prices. The biggest crash in cities like Phoenix, Las Vegas, Miami, Fort Lauderdale, and others saw prices climb sharply back. Today, home prices in Denver and Dallas are higher than ever.[3]

From the wreckage of the crash, a whole lot of money is being made in real estate. Who is stepping in to take the place of the millennials on the sidelines? It's buyers from China, South America, and Canada. Big, rich private equity firms that gobbled up apartment buildings, tracts of foreclosed homes, and large unfinished projects are either renting them out or turning them around for a profit.

Economist Peter Morici, of the University of Maryland, says that in an aging bull market in stocks, real estate is the single best investment for most people.

"If you are saving for a down payment for a house, buy as soon as you can. A home *priced within your means* remains your best, first investment. It pays dividends every night you sleep in it," he says.[4]

Table 6.2   Average Purchase Price for U.S. Homes Paid by Top Five Countries Buying Here

Canada	$314,718
China	$590,826
Mexico	$224,123
India	$459,028
United Kingdom	$499,242

Source: National Association of Realtors

Indeed, housing is the one expenditure that is both consumable and appreciable. In a perfect world, you can live in the investment and eventually make money from it.

But even as home prices and home sales have recovered over the past few years, real people aren't participating as they should be at this stage of a recovery. First-time home buyers have not been major beneficiaries of the housing recovery—at least not yet. First-time home buyers account for less than a third of home sales, down from the more typical 40 percent.[5]

The big players in the past few years have been investors, rich Americans, and wealthy foreigners. For rich international investors, U.S. real estate is the new Swiss bank account. Russian oligarchs, budding Chinese capitalists, South American moguls, and Canadian baby boomers are buying property in the United States with cash. They are plunking down hundreds of thousands of dollars to both park their money in the biggest economy on earth *and* take advantage of the relative stability of the U.S. legal system as a safe haven for their money.

The allure of buying property in the United States gets stronger by the day. Chinese buyers are the second-biggest group of buyers, but when they buy, they buy big (see Table 6.2).

"There's a kind of security to owning property in the U.S. that really doesn't exist in China," says Richard Green, director of USC's Lusk Center for Real Estate. "It is only recently that the Chinese government appropriated property pretty regularly. That means people with means are still nervous about their ability to hang on to those means if they invest in China," he says.

So smart money from around the world is flooding into U.S. housing. Economists like Peter Morici say it is the single best investment choice in the

United States today, and mortgage rates are at historic lows. Then why isn't this a gold rush for first-time home buyers? Because millennials have very different priorities, and they don't view homeownership the way the previous generation did. During the 1990s, young buyers were learning and mastering the real estate game all over the country. In cities like Chicago and Denver, condo construction exploded and the just-out-of-college crowd were getting mortgages and trading up as home prices rose.

Today, that young-potential-buyer cohort is more likely to live at home or be renters in homes shared with other people. Real estate experts contend that the way this young generation approaches homeownership will determine just how robust the real estate market is in coming years.

Real estate expert Karl "Chip" Case warned *CNNMoney* that any first-time homeowners need to be certain they can afford the house and understand they will not turn a quick profit. "If you're not buying it for the long haul, don't buy because there's a good chance you'll have to sit through some down cycles," said Case.[6]

GENERATION RENTER

You're living at home longer, you have less disposable income, you're less likely to get married, and you want different things from your job, career, and education than any generation before you. These new attitudes—in the wake of a historic real estate crash from 2006 to 2010—means you are at the vanguard of a reset of the mortgage and real estate markets.

When baby boomers were in your shoes in 1980, their homeownership rate was a robust 51.6 percent, according to analysis by real estate research firm CoreLogic. Homeownership for the same age group in 2012—your age group—dropped 14 points, to 37.9 percent. Marriage tends to drive homeownership, but you are getting married later. In the short term, the housing market may well be held back by this generational change, yet, in the longer term, CoreLogic says über-educated millennials with their higher earnings will eventually come to the real estate market.

> The rise of educational achievement has been occurring steadily and started well before the Great Recession began in 2007. Educational attainment is theoretically an investment in future income

earning capability, so the fact that millennials are more educated than prior generations should prove beneficial for their ability to become homeowners in the long term. However, in the short term, they will carry higher debt loads, and those with less than a bachelor's degree are facing stiffer economic headwinds.

—*Sam Khater, Deputy Chief Economist, CoreLogic*[7]

Those headwinds will eventually become tailwinds as millennials earn more. Harvard real estate researchers see a millennial-driven housing boom on the horizon.[8] They predict that an improving jobs market and a better economy will prod millions of millennials out of their parents' homes and right into their first mortgages, adding 24 million new households by the year 2050. The three things holding young homeowners back today—a weak jobs market for recent graduates, too much student debt, and tight lending standards—will eventually fade, setting up the housing market for a wave of new buyers.

"When the job market recovers and their income recovers, they are going to make their mark on this housing market," says Harvard's Christopher Herbert.[9]

Don't forget about generation X—those between the ages of 35 and 49, who, by and large, overpaid for their homes during the boom—working against millennials as well. Zillow says 42.6 percent of generation-X homeowners are underwater on their home loans, meaning they owe more on the home than it is worth. If they were to sell, they would have to bring a check to cover the difference between what they paid for the home and what it is worth today. It's a traffic jam for the housing market. With gen X stuck in the middle, millennials have a tight supply of starter homes to choose from and baby boomers don't have enough potential buyers to sell to (see Table 6.3).

Zillow concludes: "Bottom line, millennials have nothing to buy, Gen Xers can't sell and Baby Boomers have too few people to buy their larger homes."[10]

At some point, that gridlock will shake loose. Slowly improving home prices will help. And so will a more meaningful push from millennials to get into the housing market. You won't remain renters forever.

Melissa is in her early twenties and is just the right kind of millennial to turn from renter to real estate buyer. She uses her credit card but pays it off

Table 6.3   Homeowners Underwater (National Negative Equity)

Q2 2014	% Underwater
Overall	17
Millennial	15.3
Generation X	42.6
Baby boomers	31.1

Source: Zillow Negative Equity Report, Q2 2014

every month in full. She has student loans for her undergrad degree in psychology, but she signed for automatic payments that dropped her interest rate by 0.25 percent, to 4 percent. She's working for a software development company in Indianapolis and contributes the maximum to her 401(k). The company matches each dollar she invests up to 8 percent of her income. Because she pays her credit cards on time, every time, and she has autopayments for her student loans, her credit score is very high.

She has a healthy and realistic view of managing her debt. But because she has $70,000 in student debt, she's a few years out from buying real estate.

She doesn't regret the student loans. She views it as "good debt," not "bad debt" like credit cards. A graduate of the University of New Hampshire, she would never have been able to afford school without acquiring the debt. She smiles wryly when explaining that her major was psychology, but she's using her degree in a growing field: software development.

"For people my age, you have to consider what kind of debt it is," she explains. Credit card debt is often frivolous spending or a sign of the lack of financial discipline. Student debt was an investment for Melissa. She's paying it down religiously at 4 percent (a relatively low rate for borrowed money), and she is getting the free money that is the 401(k) match from her company. She and all her friends are renting apartments. But she is working hard toward buying a two-bedroom apartment in Indianapolis and renting out one of the bedrooms to a roommate. It would cover, she expects, a little more than half the mortgage and cost her less than her current rent. The difference would go toward an extra student loan payment every few months.

With $70,000 in student loan debt, Melissa is a few years away from her goal, but she will be part of that millennial housing boom when it happens.

Until then, she's got to live lean and pay every cent she can on those student loans. Once she has the loan balances low and a good income track record, she can start preparing for the process.

GET READY TO BUY

One Year Out:

Most buyers should start sprucing up their finances starting a year before they are ready to buy. Step one? Build savings. Cash is king, and you may have to fork over a 10 to 20 percent down payment for a conventional loan. You'll need at least 3.5 percent down for an FHA loan. Lenders will want to make sure you have plenty of cash in the bank for up to six months of mortgage payments and utilities. Lenders want to see job stability, cash in the bank, and a reliable credit history. So at this early stage, you'll need to examine the credit record the banks will see. Order your free credit history from www.annualcreditreport.com and scour it for mistakes. Fixing those mistakes may take some time but can raise your credit score immediately. (Don't click on any of the offers for paid credit score reports. Under the law, you are entitled to see your credit history for free once a year.) Make sure your finances are boring and predictable. Pay your bills on time, every time. Do not open any new credit cards or close any old ones. The best interest rates go to the highest credit scores.

Credit Score Secrets
- Pay bills on time every time.
- Go to Annualcreditreport.com to find mistakes.
- Pay more than minimums on credit cards and loans.
- The higher the score, the lower your interest rate.

Six Months Out:

Check rent-versus-buy calculators to make sure it is a better deal to buy in your area. Trulia.com analyzes loan rates, taxes, insurance, rents, and home prices in different neighborhoods. Trulia factors in how long you think you will live in the home and clearly shows whether renting or buying is the best financial decision. http://www.trulia.com/rent_vs_buy/

Another real estate tracker, Zillow.com, can help you determine how much house or apartment you can afford considering your savings, income, and other debts. Begin to look at listings in different neighborhoods in which you think you want to live to get an idea of what the market is. Keep in mind that first you need a budget for what you can afford to buy. On top of the mortgage, there will be homeowner's insurance, property taxes, utilities, and annual maintenance costs for the home. Plan on 1 percent of the cost of the home for annual maintenance, and scan real estate listings for property tax information. You can check insurance rates at www.Insweb.com. Don't stretch for more house than you can afford. Aim to keep your monthly real estate costs around 28 percent of your income. Anything more than 35 percent is too expensive.

Three Months Out:

Pick your mortgage loan. The vast majority of home buyers choose a traditional fixed-rate home loan. Fifteen-year loans have lower interest rates but higher monthly payments. Thirty-year loans have lower payments, but you'll pay a lot more over the life of the loan. Many people have no intention of staying in a home for 30 years to pay it off. If you are reasonably confident this is a starter home and you will be able to sell it and upgrade later, then a 7/1 adjustable-rate loan may be right for you. The interest rates on the loans are incredibly low for the first seven years, before adjusting sharply higher after that. It's a popular choice for young home buyers in booming markets like New York City.

You'll need to work with a Realtor you trust who has experience in your price range. Make a clear list of needs, wants, and would-be-nice-to-have features of the property you want to buy. Finally, get preapproved for a mortgage. If you have an income track record and a good credit score, this will smooth the buying process.

Home Buyer Checklist
- Do you have job stability?
- Do you have cash in the bank?

- Is your credit score above 720?
- Check rent vs. buy calculators.
- Determine how much house you can afford.
- Are your monthly real estate costs around 28 percent of your income?
- Pick your mortgage loan.

MORTGAGE RATES

Much of the action in the housing market in recent years has been investors, wealthy foreigners, and baby boomers buying homes with cash. For them, mortgage rates are irrelevant. They are coming to a property closing with a cashier's check for the entire amount. That's probably not you.

Most of us will borrow money for the first home purchase, and, depending on the mortgage rate, it makes a big difference in the ultimate cost of the property. Mortgage rates have been incredibly low since the end of the Great Recession, in part because the Federal Reserve has been stimulating the economy and keeping interest rates low to spur activity. It won't last forever. But for now, these rates are, quite frankly, once-in-a-lifetime lows. The Federal Reserve is expected to slowly start raising its benchmark rates.

There are numerous resources for mortgage rates. Bankrate.com lists the going mortgage rates based on the duration of the loan and your credit score. Remember, the best rates go to the highest credit scores.

Another variable is where you will buy a home. Rates can vary by region. The biggest complaint of potential home buyers trying to nab these low interest rates to borrow for a home is that the banks are quite stingy with the deals. You'll need a credit score above 720, a 20 percent down payment, a solid and consistent job history, and a house priced right for the neighborhood. Anything less, and the bank may well deny you a mortgage.

The sad fact is that it was too easy to get a mortgage for too long, and now it is too difficult. That's the nature of the cycle. Nabbing these incredibly low interest rates takes some planning. Timing is critical. If interest rates begin to rise, so will the cost of homeownership. In the spring of 2014 the median price of an existing home was $212,400, up 4.4 percent from the prior year.[11]

Table 6.4   Median Family Home Price, at Different Mortgage Rates

Mortgage rate (%)	Home price ($)	Down payment ($)	Monthly payment ($)	Total home cost ($)
4.25	212,400	42,480	835.90	300,924
5	212,400	42,480	912.17	328,381
5.25	212,400	42,480	938.30	337,788

Source: Bankrate.com mortgage calculator

Table 6.4 shows how even slight increases in mortgage rates affect the monthly payment and the total cost of a typical home.

LOCATION, LOCATION, LOCATION

Where you buy a home is critical. A community with above-average jobs growth, population growth, affordable housing stock, and a diverse employment base is a thriving place for millennial homeownership. A report from the National Association of Realtors on the best markets for young people found 10 vibrant cities with good job prospects and decent housing (see Table 6.5). Texas is growing like gangbusters, and, on average, 110 people move to Austin every single day, many of them under 35 years old. In Grand Rapids, Michigan, job creation is above average and just about a third of new residents between 2010 and 2012 were between the ages of 24 and 35. Des Moines has affordable housing stock, stable insurance and finance jobs, and a thriving start-up scene.

Table 6.5   Best Cities for Millennial Home Buyers[12]

City	Median home price	Job growth
Austin, TX	$226,000	4.2%
Grand Rapids, MI	$123,000	4.2%
Dallas, TX	$175,000	3.9%
Des Moines, IA	$153,000	3%
Ogden, UT	$184,000	2.7%
Denver, CO	$288,000	2.7%
Seattle, WA	$340,000	2.6%
New Orleans, LA	$158,000	2.5%
Salt Lake City, UT	$233,000	2.4%
Minneapolis, MN	$188,000	1.5%

AFFORDABILITY

Housing costs for both renters and buyers have been rising faster than wage growth during the economic recovery, and economists predict that trend will continue. Rent is currently more expensive than ever in many metro areas, according to Zillow, making it harder for renters to save for a down payment on a home down the road.

"As rents keep rising, along with interest rates and home values, saving for a down payment and attaining homeownership becomes that much more difficult for millions of current renters, particularly millennial renters already saddled with uncertain job prospects and enormous student debt," says Zillow's Humphries. "In order to combat this phenomenon, wages need to grow more quickly than they are, particularly for renters, and growth in home values will need to slow."[13]

$65,514

The median income of a homeowner,[14] compared with $31,888 for renters.

LIVING AT HOME

When it comes to living at home when you are loaded with debt, it's worth repeating: *Do it!* Thankfully, for millennials, there is little stigma to the "living-in-your-parents'-basement" stereotype, especially among their peers. For generation X, living at home was a relationship killer and a sign of failure to launch. Now, it is the single best personal finance move many young people can make.

Rising rents and declining rent affordability are good reasons to stay at home as long as you can, especially if you live in the high-cost Northeast and on the West Coast.

I suspect that millennials will be more sensible and less credit-addicted than generations before. Studies repeatedly show that the younger generation cares about how they spend their money and what it gives them in return. You expect more out of your jobs, careers, and relationships, and that 1990s pursuit of square footage and material possessions seems downright passé. In a way, computer and cell phone technology have given us creature comforts that we could not have imagined 20 years ago. It is my hope that this reverses an acquisitive trend in the United States.

What was that trend? Over a 20-year period, Americans moved into bigger homes and moved farther away from their jobs. They spent less time at home, built more garages than there were drivers in the household, and bought more cars than there were people to drive them. U.S. families added media rooms and craft rooms and extra bedrooms. The "great room" was invented to coexist with the family room, the living room, and the finished basement. The average size of a home jumped 49 percent in a generation.[15] With it, came higher heating bills, higher credit card bills for filling that house with stuff, and longer commutes. It also meant that it took two incomes to afford that house. (Admit it, these are your parents.) In 1970, U.S. Census data show that a single-family home in the United States was 1,525 square feet. By the peak of the housing bubble, new homes were a whopping 2,277 square feet. That, indeed, was the late-twentieth-century and early-twenty-first-century American middle class—an economic mirage housed in homes larger than families actually needed, paid for on credit, and betting that it could all go on endlessly.

What's fascinating about you millennials is that your generation seems to reject all that. You don't want quantity. Studies show you want quality; you want rich experiences, freedom, and flexibility. I am betting the middle-class dream of the 1980s through the early 2000s—paid for with plastic—is not your dream.

Chapter 6 Action Plan

Rents are rising across the country. Most millennials are paying up to half their income on rent. Aim to whittle that down by doubling up with roommates or living at home. Mobility is key for you if you need to move for a job. Be ready to relocate where the jobs are: Austin, Des Moines, Denver, Seattle. Mortgage rates are near rock-bottom, and home prices are almost 20 percent down from their peak. This is a powerful combination for buying a home. If you have low debt, a good credit score, and enough cash for a down payment, check the rent-or-buy calculators to see if buying is right for you. Here are some critical considerations:

- Will you live in the home at least seven years?
- Is the commute to work short?
- Will total housing costs be less than one-third of your take-home pay?
- Could you sell or rent the home if you moved for your job?
- Are the schools good? (Important for resale value.)
- Is the size of the home reasonable? Don't buy the biggest house on the block.
- Can a friend rent a bedroom and help with costs?
- If your significant other is moving in, will he or she kick in a portion of the rent/utilities/upkeep? Put that in writing.

CHAPTER

Family Money

23%

Percentage of couples who say talking about money would lead to a fight, reveal unwanted secrets, or cause them to break up.[1]

Families are not very good at talking about money. We never have been, really. Whether saving for college, paying for a wedding, or periodically adjusting financial goals, it's a scary, taboo subject mostly avoided. Perhaps it is perceived as crass to talk about how much money you have and what your wealth goals are. Or maybe there is embarrassment about *not* having financial goals. Whatever the reason, we're more likely to talk about religion, politics, and sex than money. We'd do well to spend less time arguing about politics and more time having frank discussions about finances.

For millennials, money discussions come in three varieties. First, with their parents there are conversations about who's paying tuition or cosigning student loans. Living at home? Will the boomerang back to the childhood bedroom come with strings attached and, if so, what are they? What is the proper way for a college graduate to ask for money? And, most important, are the parents being clear with their child about whether their own retirement savings are being used to pay for the millennial's launch into the world? (Read on.)

The second discussion is among peers. Are you sharing the expenses for dinners out and concerts? Trading off? Imagine three friends are sharing a one-bedroom apartment. Have you worked out who is sleeping on the couch and who is sharing the bedroom? Will you rotate? Will one person pay more than the other? And is there an agreement for when one renter's boyfriend shows up and stays there for days or weeks on end?

The third mandatory conversation is among couples—both nascent and established.

Let's start there. Consider this (true) scenario: The 30-year-old groom-to-be sits down with his prospective bride to sign a lease for a car. In this process he finds she has $65,000 in student loans and $13,000 on credit cards. He's floored that she (1) has that much debt and (2) never mentioned it. The more she downplays the debt, the more concerned he becomes. He could understand the student loan debt. But the credit card debt is a real turnoff. The more he obsesses over it, the more she thinks he is too materialistic.

The topic of her debt dominates the bachelor party, and even as he walks down the aisle the groom's friends are taking bets on how long the marriage will last.

Prudent? Or heartless? Maybe a little bit of both.

Couples and money has always been a combustible subject, but the current trends of rising student loan debt and a slow jobs market for graduates add new fuel. Couples counselor, psychologist, and author Jeff Gardere tells me that, in this case, the bride should pay all her premarriage debts on her own.

"If she really loves him, she will do better and pay her bills on time. If he really loves her, he should teach her how to be more financially responsible," Gardere maintains. Of course, that means talking about money and that is something couples of all ages are not very good at. An astonishing 45 percent of couples said talking about money before marriage would be "awkward," according to the National Foundation for Credit Counseling. Gail Cunningham, the NFCC spokesperson, advises couples to "talk before they walk."[2]

DATING AND MONEY

> "Women are coming to the table with some powerful resources and are looking for a financial partner."
> —*Relationship expert Wendy Walsh*

The real question? How could you be so close with someone and never have money and debt come up in conversation? With all the information available about a partner—from snooping around their social media footprint, for example—why are young people more likely to ask about old boyfriends and girlfriends (something that doesn't matter) than about finances (something that does!)?

"Because we still do not have financial literacy as we should in our culture," explains psychologist Gardere. "I honestly think it is easier and less complicated for people to talk about sex than money. Besides, talking about sex does not translate into commitment and a future. Talking about money does."

Relationship expert Wendy Walsh is even blunter.

"Sadly they are not even asking any of these questions. What people are doing now is signing up for these low criteria relationships to keep their options open. Most of the relationship takes place via technology. No one is doing a courtship dance," she says.

She looks at it from the perspective of young women, who have gained unprecedented economic power over the past two generations: access to and success in college; a place in all corners of the jobs market; key positions in banking, technology, and government.

Yet talking about money in a relationship is a minefield.

"We have this problem, we label women gold diggers if they ask about money," Walsh says. "It is actually the opposite. Women are coming to the table with some powerful resources and are looking for financial partners."

The frank Walsh, who counsels couples on money, says healthy young couples should heed the three "F's" of a relationship, as she puts it: feelings, finances, and *then* intimacy.

"The conversations people should be having before the onset of sex are critical," she says. "When you get in a love relationship with somebody, of course you are concerned about their ability to exchange care with you—their compassionate intelligence. But you are also looking at their financial intelligence. If they can carry a lot of debt cavalierly and you can't, it is not a match."

Talking about money takes tact, so what is the graceful way to ask a potential mate about their money habits?

Gardere has these ground rules: "Don't ask how much they make, or how much they have in the bank. That is too personal for casual dating. Instead you can discuss broader financial goals, beliefs, feelings about money."

Someone else's money situation is none of your business until, of course, it is clear you might merge your businesses. Then you should care. I would add, it's not necessary to know exactly how much debt someone has, but tens of thousands of dollars in high-interest credit card debt or a rock-bottom credit score can be a huge red flag.

"Someone with a low credit score is someone who has trouble keeping their word," Walsh says.

Indeed, there's at least one dating website that allows users to sort by credit score and to screen out candidates with too much student debt. Of course, people don't wear their credit score embroidered on their collar. And asking someone when you first meet, "Hey, are you going to be a financial drag or a financial help if we hook up?" is just ludicrous. But don't close your eyes to context clues about a person's financial personality. By the third date, the financial picture is likely taking shape. Are you splitting the bill for dinner, drinks, or a movie? Was there grad school? Are there roommates? Living at home? (Again, the best financial decision a young person can make is living at home and saving money. Chances are, your parents live in a house that is 20 percent bigger than the typical home a generation ago. There is space. Save your money. Don't count someone out because they live at home. I see it as a sign of financial strength.)

A little observation goes a long way when meeting someone new. But what do you *do* with that information? Couples therapists say the root of many problems in a relationship is, no surprise, money.

"Often financial issues can be tied to personality issues," says Gardere. "If you are disorganized, in denial, self-medicating with spending, grandiose, take on more than you can chew, then you will have financial issues. That being said, even emotionally healthy people can get into trouble when it comes to money; after all, we are still emerging from a recession."

Is it ever okay to dump someone because you find out they are bad with money?

"It's not wrong, but it's not nice, either," says Gardere. "You could give them a chance to rehabilitate. Maybe they can fix the problem psychologically and financially. Maybe they are immature or illiterate, but are really good people otherwise. If they are incorrigible or don't really care to change, or they have deeper emotional issues that translate to money issues, then it is acceptable to move on. But also tell them why you are moving on."

No question, money habits *can* change, so it's not wise to give up right away on a potential Ms. or Mr. Right because of some unpaid bills.

MONEY HABITS OF UNHAPPY PEOPLE

Too much debt
Not enough talk
Mismatched goals
Hiding credit card spending
Resents others' financial success

"It's also possible to become a saver," says financial planner Stephanie Genkin. Recent converts can be among the most dedicated.

"I worked with a young woman who had no debt but liked to treat herself to expensive new clothes and books every month," Genkin says. "We talked about what it would be like for her to scale back on her spending in order to put away a little money each month for retirement and a rainy-day fund. I got through to her by telling her what her life might be like 10 to 20 years from now without savings. She now contributes 3 percent to her 401(k) and automates a fixed amount of her paycheck to a savings account."

Her old behaviors would have been a dating red flag. With a little encouragement, Genkin's client now brings a lot to the financial table.

THE "TALK"

Chances are, you'll have "the talk" more than once.

It's become normal—even routine—for a 21- or 22-year-old to begin life with a small fortune in student loans that must be managed properly from the start. The normalcy of that debt is actually changing how we date, whom we marry, and when we start a family. Millennials are living at home to pay off their loans (one of the smartest ways to get ahead quickly). They are renting longer and delaying homeownership because their number one financial priority is paying off the past before investing in the future.

First, the marriage stats: Millennials are saying no to marriage. The Urban Institute says today's young adults are on track to have the lowest marriage rates by age 40 of any generation before them. If the trend continues, 30 percent of millennial women will remain single by age 40, double the share of generation X.[3]

Here's why: The social importance of marriage has been declining for years. The stigma against living together outside of wedlock is evaporating, and more couples are living together instead of marrying; more women are focusing on careers first and having babies later in life. And more couples are having those children and raising families together without getting married. Demographers say marriage is no longer the launching point for adult life for many millennials.

That means many millennials will be out in the dating pond a little longer that gen X was. That's a lot of frogs to kiss.

There is no script for how to have the talk about finances, and there is some disagreement among couples counselors. What they do agree on is that money is at the root of just about every problem couples have.

Psychologist and couples therapist Gardere does not suggest talking about how much money you make specifically. It's too easy to come off as crass or materialistic. It can backfire. Instead, he says, talking about future wealth goals and how close you are to achieving them is a safe way to start.

Relationship expert Walsh suggests being open about money first and leading into a dialogue along these lines:

> You know I have worked really hard in my life and I am proud. I make XXX and I don't have any debt. I am looking for a fair partner and I am just wondering if you are able to talk about these things.

"There is nothing more attractive to both genders than someone who has some boundaries and self-respect," Walsh says. And you don't have to be deadly serious when you start the conversation. When you broach the subject of finances, "you can be flirty when you are having this conversation."

Each situation is unique, but the common thread is talking more about your goals and hopes in the beginning, so money isn't an issue later on.

Going back to those marriage stats, the subject of money matters even if you don't think you are going to tie the knot. Consider the bright young fashion assistant with no student debt, living in an expensive city, working at an exciting job, and rising quickly. Her boyfriend is a junior banker at a prestigious firm, making six figures but paying off an Ivy League M.B.A. He's got zero discretionary income, because he is (smartly) paying down his debt as fast has he can—more than half his (substantial) take-home pay goes to this. He pays half the rent, but she (who makes considerably less but has no debt) picks up the tab for dinners, dry cleaning, groceries, even plane tickets to their friends' destination weddings.

It's a good balance until they break up. She has entirely financed the relationship, and he has had a free ride to clear up his debt.

She's an example of what is often missed in the handwringing over student debt. Almost a third of students graduate with no debt at all. Their parents saved, the student worked and saved, and they earned scholarships and grants.

Some families make saving for college a huge and early priority. For those with the means, this sends their child off into the world without the huge burden the other two-thirds of graduates have. Those kids start with a decided financial advantage.

It's creating a millennial version of the "haves" and the "have-nots." Imagine when debt-ridden Alyssa meets debt-free Adam, and Adam's parents have money.

Some parents who paid their kids' way through college are insisting their debt-free kids agree to "education prenups" if they marry a partner with a lot of debt. The theory? They scrimped and saved to pay for tuition or insisted their child go to a state school instead of an expensive private school. (Or they just had more money.) They do not want their debt-free graduate to absorb someone else's debt. If their kid helps pay the student loan bills for the spouse and then the marriage breaks up, they want to make sure their child's payments to the student loan fund are credited back when the marital property is divided.

The in-laws of one of my colleagues actually paid off the debt of their new daughter-in-law so that the young couple would not be held back and could buy an apartment. But if the marriage doesn't work, the daughter-in-law has to pay it back.

It's a great deal if you can take it and if you can deal with the prenup baggage, but unless you are in the coveted 1 percent of richest households, it's unlikely a wealthy in-law is bailing you out. More likely, you both have debt, or one of you has a little debt, and no sugar-daddy in-laws are waiting in the wings to pay it off.

WHAT KIND OF DEBT?

So you're finding the context clues in the relationship, or maybe you have had the talk and find that your money views are simpatico. What do you *do* with this information? So many of the young people I interviewed in doing research for this book were very forgiving of student debt. It's the oxygen by which so many of them can go to college, so there is almost zero hesitation about dating someone with debt. (In fact, no one really asks.) A run-of-the mill $20,000 in student loans? No problem. And many of them don't want the other person across the table judging *them* because their parents couldn't put three kids through college at $25,000 a year.

A grad school debt that amounts to $80,000? Seen by most as an investment in a future higher salary—these people will be veterinarians, surgeons, bankers, and other professionals. But credit card debt? That's where money-agnostic millennials start to pay attention.

Noreen, a 25-year-old actress in Los Angeles with a "modest" amount of student loan debt she is paying off, says she is more "shocked" when potential suitors tell her they *don't* have student debt.

"Whether they just paid it off or got a free ride to college—'I treat this person like a plane crash survivor'. *But,* if the person's in debt from something *other* than education, such as going over on your credit card [by] $15,000 ... that's a deal breaker," she told me.

The National Foundation for Credit Counseling surveyed its members and found that people are more embarrassed to admit how much they owe on credit cards than their age or weight.

I'd be most embarrassed to admit my . . .

Age 1%

Weight 12%

Credit card debt 37%

Bank balance 10%

Credit score 30%

None of the above 9%

The great news is millennials are thrifty. Only 6 percent of millennials have two or more credit cards,[4] and they like to save money. It's a cocktail for financial happiness, as long as they pay their student loans and are also investing for the future.

Research by Jeffrey Dew at the National Marriage Project shows that high levels of consumer debt—such as credit card debt—actually make couples unhappier, "eroding the quality of married life."[5]

Dew says that fighting about money is the third leading cause of divorce, after infidelity and drug or alcohol abuse. And he says happy couples don't necessarily make more money than unhappy couples; they just have less debt. In fact, couples who make a lot of money but have a lot of debt are less happy than couples who earn modest salaries but are debt-free.

The warning sign is overt materialism.

> Materialistic spouses are . . . more likely to suffer from marital problems. Some spouses base much of their happiness and self-worth on the material possessions they accumulate. This materialistic orientation has implications for their marriages. Materialistic individuals report more financial problems in their marriage and more marital conflict, whether they are rich, poor, or middle-class. For these husbands and wives, it would seem that they never have enough money.
>
> —*Jeffrey Dew, "Bank on It: Thrifty Couples Are Happiest"*

For young people thinking more about the now than the happily ever after, it might feel irrelevant if your significant other is materialistic or a sloppy bill payer. But the research is pretty clear: The fewer surprises about money in a relationship, the better.

We're all wired a little differently about money. Some people are natural spenders. Some are savers—to a fault. (Be honest: You know someone who can afford to open up the wallet a little when you're all out on the town, but won't!).

My sister and brothers and I have the same parents and identical upbringing, but we all have different relationships with money. When we were little, my mom would give us each the same small sum to spend when we went to the mall. My sister would spend it on the very first thing she saw—usually candy. My one brother would put the money in his pocket and save it. He never bought anything. Not once. I would spend a half hour looking carefully for what I wanted, and either save the money to buy something more expensive the next time or carefully pick out a Barbie dress. My youngest brother would somehow convince my mom to buy him something and he'd keep the money.

How did we turn out? My sister—who splurged on candy—is now the best budgeter I have ever met. She is scrupulous with her goals and never strays. My one brother is a saver and investor, and my youngest brother works in finance. Fiscally conservative by nature, I have learned over the years to take more risk.

Variety is the spice of life, as they say, and savers and spenders together can be a great combination. With your savings you need a little bit of risk to grow wealth.

To be honest, my own marriage is a combination of no debt and gobs of grad school loans. My husband went to Catholic schools all the way through college and then grad school at New York University (NYU), taking on student loans along the way. My path was totally different: public schools all the way through college paid for by my parents with one small loan for a study-abroad trip that I paid off shortly after graduating. It wasn't until we decided to get married and joined finances that we were able to pay off his loans. But we saw my husband's student loan debt as an investment, and we were able to get out in front of it together. We talked about it, set goals, and laughed a lot about how we were so different in our outlooks. But we took it on together and had fun tracking our progress. The irony is that, over the years, he has become more conservative about his spending and I have definitely loosened the purse strings. (I blame his sisters!)

So dollar signs, credit scores, and debt loads are something to talk about and work on together. Savers are attracted to spenders, and vice versa. This means having the talk—early and often.

Money Talk Dos and Don'ts

- Do make the talk casual and respectful of different opinions.
- Do be honest about your current situation. If you make it seem rosier than it is and later on the truth is revealed, you'll lose trust.
- Don't hide income or debt. This is known as financial infidelity, and it is fatal to relationships.
- Do probe to understand long-held financial attitudes. These can come from the way someone was raised. Good or bad money DNA can be passed down. Unlike genetic DNA, it can be changed.
- Do talk about savings. How much are you saving, and what is it for? Keep the conversation positive and forward looking.
- Don't blame. It's a colossal turnoff.

Source: Gail Cunningham, National Foundation
for Credit Counseling

PIGGY BANK PARENTS

If you've been following my advice so far, and you are living at home while paying off debt and saving money, the financial relationship that matters most is with your parents. You're at a bit of a disadvantage, because they hold the cards. But there are important ways to show them that you are grateful and building toward a financial future.

First, if you are employed, consider paying even a nominal fee to them in rent each month. If they are not using their retirement to support you, they can put your "rent" aside for you as a future deposit for an apartment. You are saving for the future, and they are seeing evidence of financial responsibility. If they *are* diverting what they should be saving toward retirement to support you, then they should keep the rent. You can buy groceries, or pay the cable bill, but do something to show your gratitude and to pull some financial weight. The cardinal rule of personal finance is to never sacrifice your own retirement to pay for things for your adult children. After the Crash of 2008 and the Great Recession that followed, many families have been ignoring that rule.

Which brings me to the other "money talk." Be frank with Mom and Dad about how well *they* are saving. You have time to save and build; they do not. Be respectful of their goals. Living at home is a mostly financially painless act of generosity on their part. But don't push it. If your parents are cutting it too close and not saving for retirement, you have no business asking them for money or loans. They might love you too much to admit it. Don't take advantage.

They might be on the hook for you in ways you never imagined. If you have tons of student debt—and if any of those loans are in their names—they have to pay those loans back if you die first. Financial planners suggest talking with your parents about having life insurance on you—in case something happens to you.[6] It's a gruesome conversation, but it has happened. Parents who cosigned loans for their children had to pay off the loans when their adult children died before paying off the loans themselves.[7] Federal student loan debt is forgiven when the borrower dies, but not so private student loans. This should be a reminder to get as much federal aid first, before resorting to private lenders.

FRIENDS AND FINANCES

After college, you'll have friends in various stages of employment at different earnings levels—your friend the young social worker and your friend the (indebted) investment banker and the artist and the writer and the frustrated bartender who wants a job in fashion. Pick your scenario. It's an exciting time starting out, but it takes patience when paying the dinner check.

Betty, a 24-year-old nanny in California, draws the line between close friends she trusts and for whom she will pay and anyone else.

"If it's someone we don't know that well and they do it more than once, we cover it for them and then stop inviting them out," she told me.

This is good advice that I totally agree with. Best to be forgiving and understanding if someone is in a pinch. A good friend: Cover his dinner if he's short on cash. But if it is an acquaintance and it keeps happening, best not to enable. Again, your friends' money issues are not your deal, until you keep picking up the bill.

The situation gets even trickier with roommates. There is always the nightmare scenario of a roommate who acquires a boyfriend or girlfriend they didn't have when they moved in, which means you get a new roommate you didn't sign up for! Again, be ready to have the money talk with your roommates. In fact, it's always best to go into a roommate situation with a clear understanding of what you all agree is acceptable—laying out hypothetical situations so you have your bases covered. If it's not already spelled out or clear walking into a new roommate situation, be sure you make it so. You can even draw up a contract outlining the verbal agreement so everyone takes it seriously.

Sometimes that is already taken care of in a sublet scenario. But I highly recommend getting ahead of the situation if the terms for sharing living space are at all unclear. Life is tough enough. The last thing you need is a freeloader in your small apartment eating your food!

CROWDFUND OUR WEDDING

47%

Forty-seven percent of millennials spend at least half their paycheck on paying off debts.[8]

When you're paying almost half your income to financing debt, it leaves less money for the big stuff, and very little room for anything other than the basics.

So how in the world do you pay for a wedding?

Millennials are turning away from the large weddings their parents had and instead are choosing destination weddings to cut down on the sizable invite list and pressure that come with hometown weddings. Thousands of couples are asking their wedding guests to help fund their weddings instead of buying gifts listed on a registry. Since 2010, some 1,500 "Dream Wedding" campaigns have been launched on crowdfunding site GoFundMe.

GoFundMe would not provide fund-raising totals to *CNNMoney* but said that more than 16,000 donors have contributed to these wedding and honeymoon fund-raising campaigns. Some campaigns can attract thousands of dollars, but many receive only a few hundred, if any money at all. It's certainly an option to go this route, but it's no sure thing and does come with the potentially uncomfortable burden of asking family and friends to help foot the bill.

Chapter 7 Action Plan

Decide right now that talking money with your family and friends is not a taboo but a must-have conversation on a regular basis. Bring up the subject with your partner at a relatively early stage in your relationship.

Be casual—and *honest*—about it. You don't need to see the bank account, but get a handle on the state of his or her finances and factor it into your decision about the long-term viability of your relationship. Maybe it doesn't matter to you. But at the very least the financial health of your partner should *not* be a surprise. Have similar discussions with your parents if you are relying on them for support. Find out if they are robbing their retirement savings to help keep you above water. And be prepared to have frank talks with your friends.

Understanding Investments

31%

Share of 18- to 29-year-olds who are already saving for retirement.[1]

The secret to investing for young Americans is a four-letter word: *time*.

You've got it. And, according to Bankrate.com, nearly one out of every three of you has already started investing.

In Chapter 1, you learned about those 401(k) millionaires Fidelity has studied. Their habits were simple. They saved 14 percent of their pay every year, they took advantage of their company's match, and they were not too conservative with their investments.

There are three steps to building peace of mind and wealth: budgeting, saving, and investing. Once you have paid off your high-interest debts and built at least six months of savings, it is time to start investing.

Financial planner Doug Flynn, from Flynn Zito Asset Management, embraces the strategy known as 70-10-10-10. Live on 70 percent of your earnings. Save 10 percent. Invest 10 percent. And give 10 percent to charity or your community.

The first thing to understand about that 10 percent you'll be investing is the mix. You'll want stocks, bonds, cash, and alternative investments. (Financial advisers call this mix *asset allocation*.)

The younger you are, the more of your retirement money should be in owning shares of publicly traded companies—or stocks. A savings account may feel safe, but in a world with low interest rates, the low returns are punishing. You'll need a rainy-day fund of three to six months of savings (addressed in Chapter 1) in the bank. Beyond that, your money should be working for you, not sitting in the bank.

You have a longer time horizon to ride out the ups and downs of inevitable stock market peaks and valleys. Since 1926, the Standard and Poor's (S&P) 500 index of stocks—the bellwether of the broad stock market and a benchmark for your stock investments—has returned 10.2 percent on average, including stock gains and dividends.[2] Or think of it this way: If you invest $200 a month in an S&P 500 index fund beginning at age 20, by the age of 80 that nest egg is worth almost $5 million.[3]

It pays to save early and save a lot.

The accelerator here is called *compound interest,* which Albert Einstein is widely quoted as having called the "eighth wonder of the world." The magic of compounding is what makes *time* a four-letter word of the very best kind.

WHAT IS: COMPOUNDING

Compounding takes place when profits from an asset are invested again, or reinvested, magnifying the profit for an investor by a factor of *x.* It is also referred to as *compound interest.*

Consider hypothetical investors Susan, Bill, and Chris (see Figure 8.1).

Susan invests $5,000 a year, starting at the age of 25 and stopping when she is 35. Bill also invests $5,000 a year but starts when he is 35 and keeps investing until he is 65. Chris starts investing young—at age 25—but keeps investing $5,000 annually until he is 65 years old.

The difference is remarkable. Susan has more money than Bill, even though Bill saved for 30 years and Susan saved for only 10. And Chris blows everyone away. He followed the surefire, get-rich-not-so-quick plan for building wealth. He started early and saved for a long time.

Yet so many young people feel as though they don't have the vocabulary to speak investments, the cash flow to put something away every month, or

RETIREMENT
INSIGHTS

Benefit of saving early

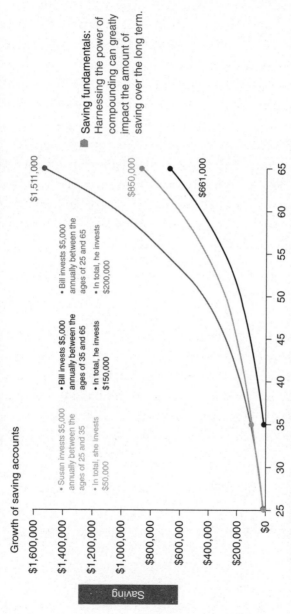

Growth of saving accounts

Susan invests $5,000 annually between the ages of 25 and 35
• In total, she invests $50,000

• Bill invests $5,000 annually between the ages of 35 and 65
• In total, he invests $150,000

• Bill invests $5,000 annually between the ages of 25 and 65
• In total, he invests $200,000

$1,511,000

$850,000

$661,000

■ Saving fundamentals: Harnessing the power of compounding can greatly impact the amount of saving over the long term.

The above example is for illustrative purposes only and not indicative of any investment. Account value in this example assumes an 8% annual return.
Sources: J.P Morgan Asset Management.
Compounding refers to the process of earning return on principal plus the return that was earned earlier.

Figure 8.1 Savings of Hypothetical Investors

Source: JPMorgan Asset Management, Retirement Insights Benefit of Saving Early

the confidence to put their time advantage to work. That goes for every generation when they were young—but it's even more complicated for millennials, aka "Generation Recession." Survey after survey shows that you millennials are cautious and conservative in investing. Yes, you are saving and are frugal (bravo!), but you are shy about investing. That may hold you back.

Among all investors, you have the time to ride out the ups and downs.

Think of those lottery slogans: "You've got to be in it to win it!" "You can't win if you don't play!" While playing the lottery is a waste of money and a sure sign of a lack of financial discipline, I find the slogans useful from an investing perspective. We've just lived through one of the most lucrative six-year periods in stock market history, yet just about half of Americans don't own stocks.[4] An incredible 36 percent have no retirement savings whatsoever.[5] After the stock market crashed in 2008, investors of all ages were scared to death about losing more money in stocks, even as reasonable, seasoned veterans counseled that big dips are big buying opportunities.

> You've got to be fearful when others are greedy, and greedy when others are fearful.
>
> —*Warren Buffett*

From March 9, 2009, to August 2014, the S&P 500 rocketed 195 percent higher. What happens next is yet to be written, but what has already happened is extraordinary. There will be more peaks and valleys to come and hindsight is always 20/20, but what an incredible wealth-building opportunity this has been. Investors who have been too cautious for their age and their time left until retirement missed a golden opportunity and will work longer to make up for it.

$2,945

ROMANS' NUMERAL

What a $1,000 investment made in the S&P 500 in March 2009 was worth five years later.

I don't expect anyone, starting with me, to be an expert stock picker. The aforementioned Warren Buffett himself has said that when it comes to the next decade in stocks, low-cost stock index funds will do just fine. You don't need to be dabbling in researching stocks or trying to time the market. Just buy the baskets of stock indexes that are already out there for good diversification and protection from swift moves in one particular stock.

GETTING STARTED: TAX-ADVANTAGED RETIREMENT ACCOUNTS

The most important investing you will do is inside a company-sponsored 401(k) or in a Roth individual retirement account (IRA) or other tax-advantaged retirement accounts. This is the money that you will set aside and grow for the long term, and that you will live off of in retirement. Leave it there. The biggest sign of economic distress is dipping into the money in your 401(k). Don't do it.

Start investing young, and be consistent. When you buy a small quantity of stocks and bonds each pay period, and put it to work, you are doing *dollar-cost averaging*. This approach smooths out the ups and downs of the market. Slow and steady wins the race. If you are consistently investing over a period of years (dollar-cost averaging) and consistently rebalancing your portfolio (sticking to your recommended asset allocation), you are on your way to a smart and rich finish.

"Retirement planning." Even the words sound old and boring! It's such a turnoff for young people, who are just starting in their jobs, lives, and adventures, to think about gray hair. Those retirement commercials on TV with the golden light, the pretty pastel vineyard scenes, and the elegant middle-aged couple living out their dreams? They don't really speak to you. But take it from me, time is more important than money in the retirement planning game, and you have plenty of time. The time to start planning for it is at least 10 years before your first gray hair.

I began investing in a 401(k) when I was 22 years old. My boss sat down with me and insisted I contribute 10 percent of my pay each month to the company 401(k). He explained that I needed 90 percent in stock index funds or diverse mutual funds with the lowest fees possible. He made sure I navigated the prospectuses online and explained that the money in those funds was never to be touched.

He wanted me to contribute even more, but I had a student loan I was furiously trying to pay off. It took me a few months, but soon the loan was paid off and I was contributing 15 percent to the 401(k).

Today, I give the same advice to young people I work with. The student loans they have are generally much bigger than those of my generation. But the advice is the same. Time trumps money.

The government is so eager for Americans to save early and often that there are tax advantages for doing it. Some retirement vehicles, such as traditional IRAs and 401(k) plans, allow investments to grow federal income tax–deferred. A Roth IRA allows the money to grow tax-free. Employees can contribute up to $17,500 of their pretax earnings a year into their company-sponsored 401(k) plans, and $5,500 for an IRA. (These are the 2014 limits and will certainly rise in coming years.) The lump sum may sound scary. "How in the world can I find 17 grand to invest?" you might ask. Think of it this way: Investing $17,000 in a 401(k) is the equivalent of about $210 a week after the pretax saving is calculated.

TIME IS A FOUR-LETTER WORD

Financial experts agree, that even though you feel like you may be too busy to spend time on investing basics, you must do it now.

I'll never forget this vivid explanation from a former financial advisor I once interviewed. She told young people that investing was as easy as dressing. "If you know how to dress, you know how to invest." Look at it this way—when you get up in the morning you put on pants or skirt and a top. If it is cold, you grab a sweater. If it rains you put on a raincoat and in the winter you wear a parka. Investing is a lot like this.

You know the basics for each season. You need to "wear" the basics of stocks, bonds, cash, and alternative investments. And every "season" you tweak the wardrobe—changing what's in your closet (portfolio) in a process known as *rebalancing*.

If managing your money seems scary or daunting, autoenroll in a 401(k) with automatic rebalancing every year to make sure the portfolio matches your desired risk and age levels. If you have a company 401(k), all this is spelled out in the plan material. Take the time to read and reread every word. Set it and forget it.

Studies show that the millennial generation is more risk averse than their parents and even their grandparents. It's natural, really. They are a generation coming of age in a time of huge stock market swings, superlow interest rates, and a job market that is less than ideal. When nothing feels certain, there are student loans to pay and the only available jobs don't need a college degree.

Yet all this is happening in the most important stage of your investing life as a millennial. Ryan Mack, of Optimum Capital Management, isolates three phases of your financial life for retirement planning purposes:

Phase 1. Accumulation: "You are in your twenties and you are young, full of vigor, and have the unprecedented ability to sustain risk," Mack says. "You have almost 40 years and multiple market cycles to go before you are going to retire. If you have a portfolio that has 80 to 90 percent in stocks and you can tolerate that high amount of risk then by all means have at it!"

Phase 2. Conservation: These people are age 30 or 40 and now have a nest egg they have been working for years to build, and they don't want to lose it. When you get to this phase, you'll start diversifying away from such a heavy stock portfolio. Mack suggests this is the phase in which to add gold to a portfolio to hedge against inflation and the possible weakening of the dollar. Mack says both of these things are possible, so he recommends a 10 percent position in a gold exchange-traded fund (ETF) and a 50 to 60 percent position in stocks.

Phase 3. Distribution: Age 50 is not the time to start paying attention to investing for the first time. Yet, frighteningly, many people enter their fifties without much saved for retirement or a 401(k) on autopilot. At age 55, Mack says a portfolio of 80 percent in stocks is too much. He recommends 50 percent bonds, 10 to 15 percent gold, and the rest a mix of stocks and international stocks.

The right mix is called your *asset allocation*, and it depends on your age, goals, and appetite for risk. For the purposes of the young investor, your asset allocation should be much heavier in stocks than bonds compared with someone older. Bonds, remember, are debt that the government and companies sell to investors with a promise to pay them back over time. Interest rates right now are extremely low, so with government bonds you are really buying the security of getting paid back; they yield generally lower risk or reward over time versus stocks.

I recommend you spend 10 minutes playing with a few online risk calculators to see what kind of investor you are. My favorite is http://money.cnn.com/quizzes/2011/pf/ultimate-portfolio-quiz/. Here are a few others:

CNN http://money.cnn.com/calculator/retirement/retirement-need /?iid=EL

FINRA http://www.finra.org/Investors/ToolsCalculators/

GetSmartAboutMoney.ca http://www.getsmarteraboutmoney.ca/en /tools_and_calculators/calculators/Pages/AllCalculators.aspx#.U _9fo0v3pFx

Vanguard https://personal.vanguard.com/us/FundsInvQuestionnaire

Rutgers http://njaes.rutgers.edu:8080/money/riskquiz/

Once you decide what kid of investor you are, you can dive in and still sleep at night. This is why Mitchell Tuchman, managing director of Rebalance IRA, breaks down investor portfolios into these categories:

- *Income*: For money that you'll need in the next one to three years for, maybe, a house down payment.
- *Conservative growth*: Let's say you have savings that you may need in three to five years, but you're not sure if you will need it before then. Until you are sure you can invest these savings for the long term, this is a place to leave money that needs to be in a "holding pattern."
- *Moderate growth*: If you are nervous about the markets and this is money for long-term retirement, this is a good portfolio to help you acclimate to market fluctuations and get your "sea legs." It isn't optimal for the long term, but if you are a nervous person, this is a good place to start so that you can see how your portfolio will recover after a correction.
- *Growth*: If you are putting the money away for the long term and you don't watch the market or get really upset at fluctuations, this is the perfect portfolio for anyone under age 45 and for most people until they are five years away from retirement.

Tuchman advises that if you have less than $50,000, pick the portfolio that best suits your life situation and invest in one of the appropriate Vanguard funds. You can buy these in any brokerage account, or you can open up an account directly at Vanguard. If you have more than $50,000, then you can build the other portfolios using the symbols listed in Table 8.1.

Table 8.1   Tuchman Portfolio

	Income	Conservative Growth	Moderate Growth	Growth
Under $50,000				
Vanguard Lifestrategy Funds - Symbol	VASIX	VSCGX	VSMGX	VASGX
Average Fund Fee	0.17%	0.17%	0.17%	0.17%
Over $50,000				
Income				
Corporate Bonds (VCIT)	40.0%	30.0%	20.0%	10.0%
High Yield Corporate Bonds (HYG)	40.0%	30.0%	20.0%	10.0%
	80.0%	60.0%	40.0%	20.0%
Equities				
US Total Market (VTI)	9.0%	15.3%	23.0%	27.0%
US Small Cap (IJR)		2.7%	4.1%	9.0%
Foreign Developed / Emerging (VEU)	9.0%	15.3%	23.0%	27.0%
International Small Cap (VSS)		2.7%	4.1%	9.0%
US Real Estate (VNQ)	2.0%	4.0%	6.0%	8.0%
	20.0%	40.0%	60.0%	80.0%
Weighted Average Fund Fees	**0.27%**	**0.23%**	**0.19%**	**0.16%**
Estimated Dividend Yield (from 2014)	4.0%	3.6%	3.2%	2.8%

Source: Rebalance IRA

If you are anything like your millennial cohort, you're pretty conservative about investing in stocks. A fascinating study by UBS found that you actually invest a lot like your grandparents.[6] Shaken by the recession, you can't tolerate a lot of risk. You have witnessed firsthand the greatest economic devastation since the Great Depression. Your parents' home value crashed. Their retirement savings dropped hard in 2009, and you personally are facing a tough jobs market. As a result, your generation is sitting on more cash than any other generation. The money is in the bank, not in a retirement account.

Investors between the ages of 21 and 36 "fully buy into the redefinition of risk as permanent loss," the UBS report revealed. And, while that seems prudent now, it means you're not taking full advantage of the time factor of investing.

Consider that you'll need about 8 times your annual salary saved in retirement funds, according to Fidelity Investments. Some financial planners urge more like 10 to 12 times your salary. Essentially, you need to save well north of a million dollars. And that's conservative. How's this for sobering: A 2013 study by the Employee Benefit Research Institute found that nearly half of all workers had less than $10,000 saved.

Peter Morici is an economist and professor at the University of Maryland known for his plain-spoken translation of the dismal science, economics.

"If you're nearing retirement, keep about half your money in cash and low-risk bonds with short maturities, and the rest in a diversified portfolio of stocks," Morici advises. He recommends an S&P 500 Index Fund offered by the credit union USAA or a similar low-cost service.

"If you're younger, set aside a reasonable amount each month to put into a similar basket of equities, stick to that discipline through thick and thin, and you'll make out just fine over the long run," he says.

And here is his most passionate admonition for young investors. "History is replete with fools who bet against the United States of America. If you permanently avoid stocks, it's not only unpatriotic, but downright dumb."

Investing Priorities

1. Have a three- to six-month rainy-day Fund of liquid savings.
2. Invest enough in the company 401(k) to get the full match.
3. Pay high-interest credit card balances.
4. Pay down private student loans.
5. Contribute more to the 401(k).
6. Pay down government student loans, car loans, and mortgages.

NO 401(K)? INVEST ANYWAY

Millions of workers do not have access to a 401(k) plan through their job. That means they don't have the free money of the company match, either. But that doesn't mean you can't or shouldn't be saving young for retirement. Remember, time is on your side. Even without a company match, even small amounts of money can grow over the years, but it's up to you. Here are your options.

Traditional IRA:

This individual retirement account allows you to get started saving on your own and brings with it some tax breaks to boot.[7] The annual contribution limit is $5,500, and if you are single without a workplace plan, it could mean more than $1,000 in tax savings. If you raid the IRA before you turn 59 1/2, you'll have to pay taxes and a 10 percent early withdrawal penalty.

Roth IRA:

Better for savers in lower tax brackets, a Roth IRA offers tax-free growth. You put your money in a Roth IRA after you've paid taxes on it. The younger you are, the better this option is because the pot of money grows for decades tax-free, avoiding a tax bill at retirement time. The contribution limit mirrors the traditional IRA, but there are income limits: $114,000 for single filers and $181,000 for married couples.If you make more money than that, you cannot contribute to a Roth. You can withdraw your contributions at any time without penalty or taxes. Early withdrawals of investment earnings on those contributions are taxable, with a 10 percent penalty.

Young people are increasingly turning to the traditional and Roth IRAs to help buy their first home. Special rules allow savers to draw on earnings from the accounts for a qualified first-home purchase (up to $10,000) or for education expenses. (You'll still have to pay income taxes.)

Rebalance IRA's Tuchman does not mince words when it comes to a Roth IRA: "Open up a Roth IRA and put as much as you can into it every year," he advises. "If you are 25 and invest $1,000 in a Roth IRA every year for 40 years (at historic market returns of 8 percent), you would have $300,000 at age 65, and by investing in bonds, you could take out $1,000 *per month* tax free!"

MyRA Accounts:

The U.S. Treasury Department hopes to expand a pilot program and allow automatic savings for workers who do not have access to company retirement plans. It's basically a government savings account that would never lose value because it is invested in bonds. The hope is to get young workers started investing and give them stability they can draw on later. If interest rates stay low, it means returns will be low, too, and likely won't keep pace with inflation.

Now that the economy is beginning to heal, smart investors need to be extra careful not to sabotage their retirement planning themselves.

No matter what your investing strategy is, you *must* pay attention to fees, which come in three forms: fund fees, fees paid to an adviser, and commissions on trades. Rebalance IRA's Tuchman notes that they are not mutually exclusive. "Make sure you add them all up. Just 1 percent in fees is huge because you can expect, based on decades of stock market returns, to get an 8 percent annualized rate of return. One percent in fees [is] really 12.5 percent of your profits! Your total fees should be under 1 percent."

Four Dumb Moves

1. **Ignoring your 401(k).** You decided what proportion of stocks, bonds, and international funds to put in years ago and have never looked at it again. By not reallocating your assets periodically, you risk getting off track from the right asset allocation for you. A young person should have more stocks and fewer bonds than someone approaching retirement. Along the way, you should take profits in the asset classes that have performed well and add slightly to the others at lower prices to keep your assets in balance and keep your money working for you. You don't have to do this every quarter. You can decide to reallocate every six months or every year. Just do it.

2. **Underestimating your health care costs.** You're in the first innings of a long and exciting life, so most people don't consider this when they are planning for the future. Nursing homes, assisted living, and so on, will not be completely covered by Medicare and Social Security. According to Fidelity Investments, you need $250,000 in retirement for health expenses outside of your retirement savings. You will spend vastly more money on health care in the last two years of your life than during the rest of your life combined.

3. **Starting too late.** $2,000 saved in your twenties is more valuable than $10,000 saved in your fifties. Here's why: the miracle of compound

interest. Using the historical rate of stock market return, that $2,000 in your twenties grows to more than $20,000 by the time you retire. Invest five times that in your fifties, and it is worth less than $18,000 on retirement. The goal is to start early and invest every year. The most important advantage you have is time.

4. **Cashing out the 401(k) early.** Here's why it is so dangerous when young people cash out the 401(k) early: They think that the few thousand dollars they have in the account is inconsequential but necessary to pay bills. Consider this: The $5,000 cashed out at age 25 is $75,000 of retirement savings you have sabotaged. A recent study by Hewitt Associates found a majority of young people cashing out their 401(k)s. Even if it amounts to only a few thousand dollars, this seriously jeopardizes retirement. When you are young, time is on your side. The longer you have to go until retirement, the more that money works for you. And cashing it out means taxes and a 10 percent penalty. So pulling out $5,000 means you'll take home half of that and rob yourself of tens of thousands of future retirement dollars. It is simply not worth it. Retirement money is for retirement, not for paying bills.

BUILDING BLOCKS

I'm the first to admit that it's daunting to get started with your investment strategy—just one look at the acronyms in the financial world can make your head spin. While there are entire books out there (and maybe my next one!) that delve deeply into the complexities of trading and the strategies behind it, let me get you started with some basic but key terms and entities to give you a foundation on which to build your investments.

What is a mutual fund?

Mutual funds are the most common investment vehicles out there. A mutual fund pools money from thousands of investors and uses it to buy a portfolio of stocks, bonds, real estate, or alternative investments, depending on the stated goals of the fund. As a shareholder in the mutual fund, you have a slice of all those investments at the same time. Most mutual funds require only a small investment to get a share. Instead of you buying lots of different stocks and securities one at a time, a trained professional does it and you buy in. It's ready-made diversification, with a fund manager overseeing it. Before you invest in a mutual fund, look up its expense ratio. It may not seem like much, but those expenses will eat into your returns.

What is an index fund?

Mutual fund managers try to outperform the stock market, The managers are paid to be smarter than their various market benchmarks—the S&P 500, the Dow Jones Industrial Average ("the Dow"), the Nasdaq, etc. Instead, these index funds exactly match the broader market. These funds are passive, not active. There is no well-paid investment manager deciding what to buy. Index funds tend to charge lower fees, and they are more tax efficient because they don't buy and sell stocks over and over; they simply track the market.

What is an ETF?

You might have heard this acronym for "exchange-traded fund" before and thought it was just another exotic phrase in an alphabet soup of financial terms. But ETFs are really a simple and streamlined way to buy or sell just about anything you want exposure to as an investor. Do you think the value of gold is going to rise because the U.S. public finances are a mess or inflation is about to rear its head? There's an ETF for that: SPDR gold shares. The ticker symbol is GLD.

Do you think stock values are going to keep rising as the global economy recovers, and you want exposure to the entire stock market? There's an ETF for that, too: Vanguard Total Stock Market, or VTI.

Are you convinced the world's hunger for oil and raw materials will only grow as middle classes evolve in China and India and the world's factories hum? How about iShares S&P Global Energy IXC?

I am not recommending these. I am a journalist, not a financial planner. But you can type those symbols into any finance website and learn more about what those funds do and how much they cost. What you buy—what you invest in—depends on what you think will happen in the world. Essentially, ETFs are the low-cost version of fancy mutual funds that have managers who are paid out of your returns to manage your money. If you want a plain-vanilla investment with low fees, ETFs are a nice way to get started investing. If you want to pay a little more for a seasoned fund manager to pick and choose stocks and bonds and other instruments in the categories you are interested in, then widely held mutual funds might be worth the price.

Thanks to technology, you have more options than ever for getting started. Companies like E*Trade, Charles Schwab, and TD Ameritrade allow you to trade stocks on your own, online. You can certainly turn to a certified financial planner or a fee-only planner, or you can take a look at many of the new businesses popping up that are app-based investment tools that allow you to manage your own portfolio. Here are just a few:

- Betterment.com
- Wealthfront.com
- Learnvest.com
- Rebalance IRA

Some call these young firms "robo-advisers" because they are mainly online, automated investment advisory firms that rely heavily on investment algorithms to make trades for customers. While you could get a live body if you wanted to, these firms are known more for their handy apps that allow users to buy/sell what and when they want from their handheld devices. The lower overhead for these firms allows them to be more competitive on the fees they charge customers.

As with anything, do your homework to decide what investment platform works best for you.

What is an IPO?

An initial public offering is more widely known by its acronym, IPO. Facebook is probably the most famous recent example. Millennial wunderkind Mark Zuckerberg starts a company, drops out of college, changes the world, then offers his private company to the public to share in the ownership. By selling shares to the public, his company raises lots more money to hire more people, buy other companies, and expand operations. This means regular people get to buy a share of the company and watch its value rise—or fall. For investors, an IPO is the starting point, the birth of the company as a public entity with a stock that trades higher or lower based on its prospects.

IPOs often have a buzzy or exclusive appeal to investors. After all, who hasn't heard of GrubHub, Candy Crush, LinkedIn, Zynga, Twitter, or Facebook? But they are the riskiest investment a regular investor can make. Check out this video:

http://money.cnn.com/video/investing/2014/03/25/candy-crush-saga -king-ipo-zynga-box-grubhub.cnnmoney/index.html

Every investor considering buying shares of an IPO should examine the company's securities filing to government regulators at the Securities and Exchange Commission (SEC). It is easy to find and tells potential investors—that's you—how the company intends to make money, who its customers are, and how much money it has on hand. More compelling is the list of risks the company, by law, has to disclose before it can sell stock to the public and take your money.

The list of risks for investors in King Digital, maker of Candy Crush, was 24 pages long.[8] Among the risks to investors cited by the company: "The growth and expansion of our business and headcount create significant challenges for our management and operational resources. We cannot assure you that this level of significant growth will be sustainable in the future." And then there was this: "We may not maintain profitability in the future."

You can learn a lot about a company by looking under the hood when it files with the government to sell stock to the public. GrubHub has revolutionized the way we order food. Its IPO took place in 2014, at which time it valued itself at $1.72 billion. The company listed nine risk factors before concluding the securities filing with this warning: "We may not be able to successfully address these risks and difficulties, which could harm our business and results of operations."[9]

Investment banks shop IPOs aggressively to high-net-worth individuals and managed funds. These are considered sophisticated investors who can identify which companies have loads of risk but also have the potential for a reward that is greater. In recent years, brokerage firms and the companies going public have worked hard to get small investors a slice of the action. Sometimes it pays off. Anyone who bought into Google's IPO in August 2004 and held the stock for a decade gained 1,000 percent![10]

Sometimes it doesn't pay off, however. Facebook's IPO was a short-term disaster. The process was designed to allow small investors to get in on the action just like the big professional traders. The small investors who bought the hype got burned. Facebook shares tumbled from the start. Those who were looking for a quick pop in the stock lost 25 percent of their investment. At its worst, the stock fell to $17 a share from the $38 IPO price. It took a year to climb back to where it started. Today, the stock is well above its debut value. You could say the "I" in IPO stands for "iffy." My advice? Wait a year and see how a company performs. Let the stock jockeys jump in and out of the shares. Watch, read up, and then invest. If you try to buy an IPO through a brokerage firm, make sure to click to the "risk" section of its filing. You might be surprised by what you see.

Any investor in individual stocks—not just IPOs—should become familiar with the SEC.gov website and read the latest company filings, issued quarterly, for key information about stocks you are interested in buying. It's your money. Know where it's going and the risks/rewards that the company is signaling to the public. If the research is too overwhelming, stick with diversified low-cost index funds or ETFs.

Chapter 8 Action Plan

After paying off high-interest credit card debt and getting student loan bills in order, it's time to live on less than you earn and start investing. Start in a tax-advantaged account. Have the right asset allocation. That means the right mix of stocks, bonds, commodities, and cash. Keep the fees to a minimum. Rebalance the portfolio regularly to make sure that the allocation is appropriate. Choose low-fee stock index funds and ETFs. The younger you are, the larger the portion of your portfolio that should be in stocks. Eventually you should craft a well-diversified portfolio of stocks, bonds, cash, and alternative investments such as precious metals and real estate.

CHAPTER

Credit Karma

63%

Six in ten millennials have no credit cards.[1]

Millennials are breaking the consumer addiction to credit cards. Good for you! For Americans over the age of 30, credit cards—and credit card debt—are the norm. But your generation, chastened by the financial crisis and scared of running up too much debt, is abstaining for several reasons. The Credit Card Accountability and Disclosure (CARD) Act of 2009 made it harder for credit card companies to give out cards with high fees and interest rates to young people. Those under age 21 need a cosigner or must show they have income. A weak recovery and student debt have young people afraid of overspending.

It's an appropriate shift in mind-set away from easy financing. The easiest way to live beyond your means is to have a pocket full of credit cards. So, for now, the caution is wise. Of those millennials *with* credit cards, only 40 percent actually pay their balance every month. Among consumers over age 30, only 53 percent pay their balance in full.[2] Credit counselors say putting away the plastic and living within one's means on cash is the surest sign of financial stability.

DEBIT CARDS

The credit rating agency FICO found that the number of young Americans without credit cards has doubled since the recent recession. They can't get credit cards as easily, and they don't want them. As a result, a dizzying array of prepaid debit cards has become the plastic of choice among the millennial generation. These are reloadable and can be tied to a bank account. You may pay a monthly fee to use the debit card, an activation fee, and an ATM withdrawal inquiry fee. The rules and fine print vary widely.

There are two drawbacks of the shift away from credit cards to prepaid debit cards. The first is that they don't provide a credit history that the ratings agencies can track. Why does this matter? It doesn't matter today if you are living at home and driving your parents' car or if you're renting a place with a friend. But someday you will need a credit review to buy a car or get preapproved for a mortgage. To finance a car or a house, the bank will want to look into your credit history to see that you have paid your bills on time. The credit card history is visible and shows your habits and consistency. The better you are at paying bills, the better you look to the car dealer or home mortgage lender. You can't establish a history like that with most debit cards. If the card is lost or stolen, there are not the same protections as a credit card or bank's ATM card.

The other drawback is the cost. The fees associated with these cards can be quite high. Pre-paid debit cards backed by celebrity endorsements have among the worse reputations and highest costs. Bankrate.com can help you find the best prepaid debit card for you, arranging the options by the fees charged for loading it, activating it, and maintaining it. It's not cheap. Basically, you are paying to use your own money. It's critical that you choose the card that has the lowest fees. As bigger financial players have begun offering these cards, the prices are coming down. But be careful. (You can find a helpful table of fees at Bankrate.com: http://www.bankrate.com/finance/banking/best-prepaid-debit-cards.aspx)

Debit cards are a financial product designed for people who have trouble qualifying for credit. For many, they may be the only option. If you can, the best option is to use cash or your bank's or credit union's debit card.

OVERDRAFT PROTECTION

$39,000,000,000

Banks made $39 billion dollars in overdraft fees in 2009, all of it for charging people who overspent their accounts.[3]

If you are using your bank's debit card, you don't want automatic overdraft protection on your account.

Until recently, it was an automatic part of your debit card. If you bought a $2.50 latte but had only $1.00 in your account, the purchase would go through. But the bank would tack on a $25 "overdraft charge" because you spent more than you had in the account. Banks played it as a helpful tool, so you wouldn't be embarrassed when your ATM or debit card was rejected for insufficient funds.

Consumers screamed about incidents like these, where they could be charged almost $30 for a latte, and Congress responded. Now you, the consumer, must opt *in* to overdraft protection. And banks are pretty pushy about trying to get you to sign up. But don't. The last thing you want is to pay the bank for letting you take out more money than you have. In some cases, credit unions have more lenient fees and terms for debit card overdraft protection. Check the fine print, but keep in mind that overdraft protection is good for the bank's coffers, not yours.

If you are using overdraft protection to help you float from paycheck to paycheck, it's time to go back to the beginning of this book and set a better budget.

SO YOU WANT A CREDIT CARD?

46 years

The time it would take to pay off $10,000 in credit card debt at 18 percent APR if you make only the minimum payment and accrue no new charges.[4]

If you want to build a credit history and know that you will pay the balance off every month, a credit card is a valuable tool for you. It is critical that you pay the balance every month and not use it to float from paycheck to paycheck or to live above your means. My smart young colleagues each have one or two credit cards that they use modestly for such things as clothes, restaurant meals, and car rentals, and they pay off the balance in full each month.

Credit experts recommend keeping the total you charge on the card each month below 10 percent of the credit limit. So if you have a $3,000 credit limit, you should charge less than $300 a month. A card with a $10,000 credit limit? You should charge $1,000 or less each month. This is known as the *credit utilization ratio*. If you routinely charge right up to your credit limit and pay it off, it looks less responsible than if you are just using some of your available credit each month. Especially if you are within a year of a major purchase—a car loan, for example—you should keep that credit utilization ratio low.

If you are paying the balance, the interest rates and late fees really don't apply to you. But familiarize yourself with the annual percentage rate (APR) and any late fees that might apply. Choose automatic bill pay, and sit back and build credit.

Here are four ways to stay on top of your credit card payments:

1. Keep total charges below 10 percent of your credit limit.
2. Pay off the balance every month.
3. Choose automatic online bill payments.
4. Know what the fees are in case you miss a payment.

Most of the concerns about credit cards have to do with the spate of hacks in the past couple of years. Just about every month it seems there is a major security breach in which millions of shoppers' card information is hacked, stolen, and sold on the Dark Web. (All of your sensitive financial information can be bought for anywhere from $50 to $125.) Your financial information is least secure on the computers of health care companies and retailers. On the other end of the spectrum, the major banks are spending hundreds of millions of dollars a year staying ahead of cybersecurity. Check your account balances often. Talk to your bank and credit card issuer about the free protections that are in place to alert you if your card has been hacked and counterfeited. You don't need fancy credit monitoring at $19 a month.

The concept of the credit card is ripe for disruption anyway. Tens of millions of consumers have had their card information breached in mega hack attacks against retailers and banks. Sales fell sharply at Target when it suffered a hit to its reputation after a hack in 2014 (and the CEO lost his job). Consumers are wary of how insecure cards are. The technology is evolving—away from the magnetic stripe to chip and pin technology. That may solve some of the security issues, but there is no question that *how* we pay for things is changing. Big tech companies have been working on the concept of the mobile wallet for years. Apple unveiled its own system in the fall of 2014. Essentially, the way this technology works is that all your bank information is in your phone, with special encryption for each transaction to make your information less hackable. Watch this space. If Apple or Google or PayPal does it right, the little plastic credit card will be as obsolete as the buggy whip.

WHAT IS THE CREDIT SCORE?

> An investment in knowledge always pays the best interest.
> —*Benjamin Franklin*

Your credit score is a report card on how you handle money. It's a three-digit number that tells lenders how likely you are to pay money back. A good score will get you better interest rates on a mortgage or a car loan. A weak score will cost you more for both. Simply put: Bad credit is expensive, and good credit makes borrowing money cheaper.

Credit scores generally range from 300 to 850. A score of 720 or higher means you have sterling financial habits. A score of 620 or lower is a sign that you've had trouble paying money back—a bank may reject your application for a new loan or a credit card or charge you a much higher interest rate.

A low credit score may even cost you a new job. Employers run credit histories when they do background checks on potential employees. Expect special scrutiny for jobs where the employee would be directly responsible for cash or budgets. Not all employers will withdraw a job offer on the basis of bad credit, but many will. They see a failure to handle one's own finances as a red flag that the employee will be unable to handle company business. If you know that you have a poor credit score, be proactive with the employer. Was it due to unpaid medical bills? A roommate who skipped out on the rent? A stolen credit card or a mistake on your credit history? Be ready with an explanation.

There are three U.S. credit reporting agencies: Experian, TransUnion, and Equifax. They keep track of your repayment history. Their reports go to another company—the Fair Isaac Corporation—which generates the three-digit score that lenders look at when you apply for a loan.

Here's how it works:

- 35 percent—the biggest part of your score—is based on your payment history. So if you want to boost your score, the first thing you should do is pay on time—or even early.
- 30 percent of your score is based on the amount of credit you use. The less available credit you use, the better. Maxing out your cards will cost you points.
- 15 percent is the length of your credit history. That means how long you've had each credit card.
- 10 percent is the type of credit. You get points for having a mix of credit and retail cards, mortgage, and student loans.
- 10 percent is new credit. Opening several new credit accounts in a short period of time could ding your score.

You usually have to pay about $20 to see your credit score. You can get it from one of the credit reporting agencies. By law, you are allowed to check your credit history for free at www.annualcreditreport.com. It won't show you the score, but it will show you any unpaid bills or sums that have been sent to a collection agency. Even diligent bill payers find mistakes on this history; those errors can take time to fix and can cost you. It makes sense to check it once a year and make sure everything is correct.

The scary fact is that the credit score is a three-digit number that could cost you—or save you—tens of thousands of dollars over a lifetime.

It *is* scary, but my advice is: Don't obsess over this number. People spend hundreds of dollars a year to see their credit score and have it monitored. This is just not necessary. Pay your bills on time every time, slowly pay down your debt, and the score will rise. So don't ignore it, but don't obsess about it, either.

For more on what is counted against you on your credit score, go to http://www.myfico.com/CreditEducation/ImproveYourScore.aspx and find tips on how to raise it.

CREDIT SCORE TIPS

Check for mistakes at www.annualcreditreport.com.

Pay your bills on time or early.
Pay down debt.
Don't open store credit cards.
Don't max out cards.
Can't do any of these? Contact a credit counselor: www.NFCC.org.

Since one of the factors in your credit score is the length of your credit history (it accounts for about 15 percent of your score), many young people think they need to sign up to a get a credit card in college so they can begin establishing their track record. It's good advice only if you can pay off the balance each month and it doesn't allow you to overspend. Otherwise, the exercise in building credit early is counterproductive, since not paying bills on time is the single biggest factor in your credit score.

Those under 21 years old need a cosigner or must show they have income. Carefully consider the liability your card might be to your parents (who have to pay if you don't) and to your credit score.

A conservative approach is to use a debit card attached to a credit union bank account for the first two years of college, and then find a low-fee credit card after you turn 21. Use it sparingly—for emergencies and groceries, for example. Never max it out, and set autopay to pay the balance each month.

EXPENSIVE CREDIT MONITORING

Chances are, you can sign up for free credit monitoring if you have used your credit card at Target, Michaels arts and crafts stores, Home Depot, or a dozen other retailers within the past 12 months. When banks, retailers, or hospitals get hacked, usually the company immediately offers "free" credit monitoring so you are alerted if your information has been sold on the Dark Web, counterfeited, and used to buy thousands of dollars' worth of goods. If credit monitoring is offered for free because someplace you have shopped has been hacked, it's fine to sign up for it. Just make sure that after a period of time you don't get charged for a renewal of the service.

What's galling about credit monitoring is that *you* shouldn't have to pay because someone else couldn't keep your information safe. It's infuriating, actually. Talk to your credit card issuer. Chase, Citi, Bank of America, and others will alert you if they see suspicious activity in your account and will often deny a purchase that looks out of character for your spending history.

Fraudsters are always trolling for your personal information—by hacking personnel records at work, by installing malware on point-of-sale software at major retailers, and by poking through your trash. If you suspect you are a victim of fraud—or you want to make sure that you won't be—request that the credit agencies place an extended fraud alert on your credit files. If anyone opens up a credit request, you will be notified. Identity theft and identity fraud are a nightmare. For more on how to protect yourself, visit the websites of the Consumer Financial Protection Bureau (CFPB), the Federal Trade Commission (FTC), and the fraud tabs of the major credit ratings agencies, which are here:

http://www.consumerfinance.gov

http://www.consumer.ftc.gov/features/feature-0014-identity-theft

https://www.experian.com/fraud/center.html

http://www.transunion.com/personal-credit/identity-theft-and-fraud
.page

http://www.equifax.com/answers/set-fraud-alerts/en_cp

Brian Krebs, the cybersecurity journalist who first discovered the Target and Home Depot hacks by monitoring Russian-language online marketplaces for stolen information, says there are two easy steps to take to protect yourself from fraud:

1. Monitor your checking and credit card accounts every week.
2. File extended fraud alerts with the credit agencies.

WHAT IS THE FED?

The interest rates you pay on borrowed money trace their roots to policy set by the U.S. Federal Reserve, known commonly as the Fed. Every time you borrow money or pay a credit card bill, the Fed is influencing how much you pay. If you're an economics or business major or one of the legions of civil libertarian fans of Senator Rand Paul (R-KY), you've probably at least *heard* about the Fed. His father, Congressman Ron Paul, wants to abolish it. The younger Paul has ranted on Twitter[5] and in numerous speeches and campaign events that the Fed is too opaque and too powerful.

Here's how it works. One hundred years old, the Fed is the architect of America's money policy. It uses the tools in its toolbox to affect everything from how much a loan costs you to the outlook for getting a job.

The Fed sets a key interest rate—the *federal funds rate*—that banks use as a benchmark for all kinds of consumer loans. Mortgages, credit cards, and auto loans are all influenced by the Fed. And the Fed buys and sells U.S. Treasuries and other bonds, which affects rates and either speeds up or slows down borrowing and lending.

The Fed has a two-part structure: The central authority is called the Board of Governors and is located in Washington, D.C. Janet Yellen is the current chair of the Fed. There are also 12 Federal Reserve Banks located around the main banking centers of the country. Big policy decisions are made by a committee that includes members of the Board of Governors and presidents of the Reserve Banks. It meets eight times a year.

Congress oversees the Fed, but the Fed doesn't answer to Congress. The Fed operates independently in order to keep politics out of the process. It has two main goals:

1. To keep the prices we pay for goods and services stable. If prices are rising too fast, the Fed can raise interest rates. That makes borrowing money more expensive, slowing the economy. Picture the Fed as being like Goldilocks—it likes the economy not too hot and not too cold.
2. To make sure everyone who wants a job has one. It's what the Fed calls *maximum employment*. The Fed can't force companies to hire. But it can use its tools to create an environment for economic growth, such

as keeping interest rates low to stimulate more borrowing by businesses, which might make them more likely to hire.

These are pretty big (and wonky!) goals, and clear evidence why the Fed is the most powerful body we don't elect.

TIME TO BUY A CAR

The Fed has kept interest rates just above zero for several years. That will eventually change, and when the Fed begins raising rates it will make it a little more expensive to borrow money to buy a car or a home. No one knows for sure when the Fed will raise interest rates, and for many years they could still remain quite low.

For most millennials, the past few years of zero-percent car financing or employee-financing terms were irrelevant. You most likely weren't in the market for a car. Auto industry experts for some time have been concerned that your generation won't have the same love affair with cars that previous generations did.

But that is changing now.

Older millennial car buyers (born between 1977 and 1994) bought 26 percent of new cars sold in the first half of 2014, slightly more than the generation X demographic, according to J.D. Power and Associates.[6]

As millennials find jobs, get raises, and "enter new life stages," as J.D. Power puts it, they'll be an even bigger driver of the car market. Unless you have a bank account full of cash, you'll likely finance this big purchase. It's why you favor smaller, more fuel-efficient cars with smaller price tags. Gen X-ers love their SUVs; millennials like their compact cars. Think Buick Encore versus Ford Focus.

Once you decide you need a car, there is a careful calculation for whether it is better to buy or lease a car. Did I say "careful"? Let me say it another way. For first-time car-buyers, the process can be particularly hairy. Here is the checklist:

1. Make sure at least six months before you want to buy a car that you have checked with www.annualcreditreport.com to see that any mistakes on your credit report have been cleaned up.

2. If you want to buy a car—and intend on financing it with the dealer—check www.bankrate.com for the going rates for your zip code.

3. Be wary of stretching the car payments out longer than three years, especially if you are buying a used car. You could still be paying off the car just as expensive repairs come up. And the longer you stretch out the loan, the more interest you will pay.

4. For a new car, remember that it depreciates the moment you drive off the lot, and it comes with more expensive monthly payments. For young first-time car buyers, often a small-car lease or a used car purchase (with low-interest financing) is the best idea. Leases do come with mileage limits and charges for wear and tear.

Here is what *CNNMoney's* auto guru, Peter Valdes-Dapena, advises: "Leasing makes sense, financially, if you know for sure you won't be keeping a car for longer than a few years. In that case, why make higher monthly payments to buy a car just to get it back when you trade it in a few years?

"If you'll be keeping the car for longer than a few years (longer than the bumper-to-bumper warranty) you should probably just buy it. You don't want to be paying for out-of-warranty repairs on the finance company's car. That's no fun," he says.

Chapter 9 Action Plan

Make it a part of your weekly routine to monitor your checking and credit card accounts. If you are worried about identity fraud, consider filing a fraud alert with the credit rating agencies and renewing it every year. (It's free and more comprehensive than any credit monitoring.) Every year get a free copy of your credit report at www.annualcreditreport.com and clean up any mistakes at least six months before a car purchase or job interview. (Yes, your future employer can peek into the files and see how well you have been paying your bills.) The biggest part of your credit score is paying bills on time. For student loans and credit cards, use the autopay feature so you never miss a pay date. Pay down debt, and don't run up to the limit on the credit cards, even if you pay off the balance every month. (It looks like you're maxing out financially—a red flag.) Prefer prepaid debit cards? Be very careful of the fees. Often, you are spending 5 to 10 percent just to use your own money. Ouch. Choose a credit union debit card, turn off the overdraft protection, and keep one credit card in your pocket if you are over 21, to start building a credit history. Charge only up to 10 percent of the limit each month and pay it off. Before long, you will have a good track record and a high credit score.

Web Resources

CHAPTER 1

www.mint.com

www.levelmoney.com

www.fidelity.com

www.ameriprise.com

www.bankrate.com

www.checkingfinder.com

www.ncua.gov

www.NFCC.com

http://www.nytimes.com/2014/01/04/your-money/household
-budgeting/review-apps-to-track-income-and-expenses.html?_r=0

CHAPTER 2

www.edvisors.com

www.finaid.org/otheraid/partnerships.phtml

www.projectonstudentdebt.org

http://money.cnn.com/2014/06/24/news/economy/college-worth-it
/index.html

CHAPTER 3

www.bankrate.com/finance/student
-loans/how-long-to-pay-off-student-loan.aspx

www.fidelity.com/viewpoints/personal-finance/how-to-pay-off-debt

https://studentloans.gov/myDirectLoan/mobile/repayment
/repaymentEstimator.action

www.consumerfinance.gov/askcfpb/641/what-public-service-loan
-forgiveness.html

http://studentaid.ed.gov/publicservice

http://files.consumerfinance.gov/f/201308_cfpb_pledge-action-guide
-for-employees.pdf

http://projectonstudentdebt.org/recent_grads.vp.html

CHAPTER 4

http://www.bls.gov/news.release/empsit.nr0.htm

http://money.cnn.com/gallery/news/economy/2014/06/11/fastest
-growing-state-economies/index.html?iid=SF_E_Lead

CHAPTER 6

www.annualcreditreport.com

www.trulia.com/rent_vs_buy/

www.annualcreditreport.com

www.insweb.com

CHAPTER 7

www.stateofourunions.org/2009/bank_on_it.php

CHAPTER 8

http://money.cnn.com/quizzes/2011/pf/ultimate-portfolio-quiz/

http://www.finra.org/Investors/ToolsCalculators/

http://www.getsmarteraboutmoney.ca/en/tools_and_calculators
/calculators/Pages/AllCalculators.aspx#.U_9fo0v3pFx

https://personal.vanguard.com/us/FundsInvQuestionnaire

http://njaes.rutgers.edu:8080/money/riskquiz/

http://money.cnn.com/video/investing/2014/03/25/candy-crush-saga
-king-ipo-zynga-box-grubhub.cnnmoney/index.html

http://money.cnn.com/tools/?iid=H_PF_QL

http://money.cnn.com/calculator/retirement/retirement-need/

http://money.cnn.com/calculator/pf/millionaire/

http://money.cnn.com/calculator/pf/retirement-fees/

http://money.cnn.com/tools/savingscalc/savingscalc.html

http://money.cnn.com/tools/retireyoung/

http://money.cnn.com/magazines/moneymag/money101/

CHAPTER 9

http://www.bankrate.com/finance/banking/best-prepaid-debit
-cards.aspx

www.annualcreditreport.com

http://www.myfico.com/CreditEducation/ImproveYourScore.aspx

www.annualcreditreport.com

www.NFCC.org

http://www.consumerfinance.gov

http://www.consumer.ftc.gov/features/feature-0014-identity-theft

https://www.experian.com/fraud/center.html

http://www.transunion.com/personal-credit/identity-theft-and
-fraud.page

http://www.equifax.com/answers/set-fraud-alerts/en_cp

Cover Letters: The Good, the Bad, and the Ugly

Can you tell which of these cover letters landed an interview and which ended up in the reject pile? These are actual cover letters from job hunters, sent to career coach Brad Karsh of JobBound. We've changed the names to protect the identities of the clueless writers and the savvy job seekers who sent them. Here's a hint: The good letters have good writing, consist of short sentences, and feel like a quick conversation or introduction. The only way to make them better would be to have an actual connection to refer to somewhere in the letter: "Jonathan Smith told me to reach out to you." (Spoiler alert: I am about to disclose the good ones and the bad ones. Skip ahead if you want to guess for yourself.)

Drum roll, please ...

Joseph's and Maggie's letters are short, concise, and interesting. Maggie was asked by so many hiring managers why a stockbroker would switch careers that she decided to answer the question right off the bat in her cover letter. She did it eloquently. The second two letters are unreadable. Pay special attention to Jason's prolific use of the name of the company he is applying to—almost as if he was cutting and pasting it into a form letter. Don't just regurgitate the resume, but tell your story. As Brad Karsh says, make it like a movie trailer to draw the recruiting director in. Read the letters for yourself to decide which are best. And, keep in mind, there are many ways to formulate a cover letter. Karsh says that you should shoot for clever but remember there is a fine line between clever and irritating. Also, many younger workers are including Twitter icons and addresses and links to their social networking profiles. It's a great idea—as long as the information at the other end of those links is appropriate for a hiring manager to see. Final tip: Avoid words like *facilitate, utilize,* and *transition* (as a verb) in a cover letter. Just say what you mean in simple, clear language.

JOSEPH TEMPLETON
102 Vanderbilt Drive • Denver, CO 89816
928.829.8611 • JOSEPH@GMAIL.COM

Gary Polecki
370001 Winson Ave.
Denver, CO 34421

Dear Mr. Polecki:

Building.

It's what I do for a living.

No, not in the traditional hammer and nail sense, but in the business sense—whether it's building a marketplace for a product I'm selling, building a series of original products, or building a business.

Six years ago, the world of internet advertising was unproven and untapped. I created a sales and marketing plan for this fledgling media, and ultimately built an incredibly strong client base and revenue stream that helped our company grow 500% in six years.

In working closely with my clients and with a project management team, I built a series of innovative programs and products that respond to an ever-changing web-based marketplace. As the technology has evolved, I've been able to adapt to the playing field.

Finally, I built a business of more than 180 clients that includes senior managers and decision makers at some of the world's largest consumer brands and advertising agencies.

I'm excited to learn more about Watta Worldwide, and I'm thrilled at the chance to build your business. I look forward to following up about the Vice-President of Marketing Services job.

Regards,
JOSEPH TEMPLETON
928.829.8611

MAGGIE PINTER
315 Garden Way • Monroe, LA 42001
854.223.1235 • MAGGIE@HOTMAIL.COM

Richard Dale
83010 Quiet Oaks
Baker, LA 29292

Dear Mr. Dale:

Why would an established stockbroker give up a lucrative career and go back to school to become an editor?

It's easy. Passion.

Finding one's true calling is much more valuable than making lots of money in an unsatisfying career. I knew from the moment I cut my first piece of film that I made the right decision. Our first school project was to cut stock with a razor; I thought they were nuts to make us do it. Once I got started, they had to drag me out of the classroom! I was hooked, and it's only gotten better.

I know that I'm a nontraditional candidate. I know I'm going to have to work hard and prove myself over and over again. At the same time, I am supremely confident that I have the skills and the desire to be successful.

When I'm in the editing room, I'm happy, passionate, and dedicated. Nothing else matters.

I look forward to speaking with you in more detail about opportunities at Strategic Solutions. I'll plan to follow up with you in a week.

Regards,
MAGGIE PINTER

Gavin Richardson
123 Lane
Mobile, AL 36608

Dear Gavin,

I think I would be a great fit for your Sales position, and there are many reasons why I should be considered for this position.

As you will see on my resume, I am currently working as a receptionist at an accounting firm near campus. I've learned how to work in a fast-paced environment and show great customer service. I've made only A's and B's in college, and I was on the dean's list for several semesters. I also was involved in several organizations on campus.

My contact told me that you need a salesperson. I am a really hard worker and I always show initiative so even though I don't have a lot of sales experience, I know I could learn quickly. It sounds like this would be a great place to start my career before I go on to work with computers.

I can't wait to hear from you. Please let me know when would be a good time for an interview. Please call anytime at 223-123-2323.

I look forward to working with you!

Thank you,
TAYLOR SIMPSON

Sarah Holliman
Director of HR
Johnson & Associates

Dear Ms. Holliman,

I am very interested in the Marketing Assistant position at Johnson & Associates. I have learned of this job opportunity from a job posting on your website.

I am currently a senior, graduating in May 2010 with a Bachelor of Science in Advertising and a minor in Economics. I am very attracted to this position at Bay & Associates from the description on the posting online. I am looking to work for a company that has a positive outlook in business for its clients and employees. I hope to learn from passionate, motivating people in my career. I believe that the creative, fast-paced, and innovative culture at Johnson & Associates is one in which I would fit into and thrive from.

As you can see from my attached resume, I held many potions in college that make me well suited for a position at Bay. I was the Vice-President of Programming for the Marketing Association where I was responsible for bringing in speakers to help educate our members on careers in marketing. I also held an internship at Windy City Fieldhouse where I spent the summer working in the marketing department. There I had the opportunity to sit in on many meetings that discussed marketing and growing the business. I also participated in a brainstorming meeting where we were looking for different ways to fix our website.

Finally I have held a job at Blue Sky Chicago where I gained experience and strengthened my skills in communicating with professionals, completing projects and in research, and planning. These positions have strengthened my interest in Johnson & Associates.

Additionally, I completed several team projects in college and am able to enjoy working with a variety of individuals. I believe that I succeed in a positive working environment where I can learn from my peers, and my strong work ethic and ability to work with others would be a great asset to Johnson & Associates.

An opportunity at Johnson & Associates would allow me to brainstorm new and innovative marketing techniques, while utilizing my creative, communication and leadership skills. I am very passionate about learning new ideas and working with people, and I believe that is what Johnson & Associates is about. Please review my resume attached to this application. Thank you for your consideration and I look forward to hearing from you regarding my application. I'll plan to follow up in a week's time.

Sincerely,

JASON SMITH

(815) 555-1212

APPENDIX C

PayScale 2014–2015 College Salary Report

All data used to produce PayScale's College Salary Report were collected from employees who successfully completed PayScale's employee survey.

Sample Size: The sample size of degree-holding, full-time, civilian employees working in the United States is 1.4 million. The sample size for each school included ranges from approximately 50 profiles to approximately 4,000 profiles, depending largely upon the size of the school.

What's New?

Unlike previous years, this report includes four types of degree holders:

Bachelor's Degree Only: Only employees who possess a bachelor's degree and no higher degrees are included. This means bachelor's degree graduates who go on to earn a master's degree, M.B.A., M.D., J.D., Ph.D., or other advanced degrees are *not* included.

All Graduates: This data set contains both those whose culminating degree is a bachelor's degree and those who obtained their bachelor's degree from the school in question and then went on to get a higher degree as well (master's degree, M.B.A., M.D., J.D., Ph.D., or other advanced degrees) from the same or a different school.

Associate Only: Only employees who possess an associate's degree and no higher degrees are included. This means associate's degree graduates who go on to earn a bachelor's degree, master's degree, M.B.A., M.D., J.D., Ph.D., or other advanced degrees are *not* included.

Data Set Characteristics

U.S. Only: All reports are for graduates of schools from the United States who work in the United States. This sample does not include U.S. territories, such as Puerto Rico and Guam.

Full-Time, Civilian Employees Only: Only graduates who are employed full-time, not on active military duty, and paid with either an hourly wage or an annual salary are included. Self-employed, project-based, and contract employees are *not* included. For example, project-based graphic designers and architects, and nearly all small business owners and novelists, are not included.

Selection Criteria for Schools: The primary criteria for inclusion in this report are that a school offers either a bachelor's degree or an associate's degree, is located within the 50 United States, and has a substantial number of graduates who work for civilian employers in the United States. Schools with few bachelor's degree graduates or few associate's degree graduates and schools that have recently begun offering bachelor's degrees or associate's degrees may not be included due to insufficient data. Additionally, for the Bachelor's Only and Associate's Only data sets, schools with a large percentage of graduates earning advanced degrees may not be included due to insufficient data.

Of the approximate 3,070 bachelor's degree–granting schools in the United States, the PayScale College Salary Report 2014–2015 includes 1,002 schools. These schools:

- Include 86 percent of schools with over 5,000 undergraduate enrollment
- Include 56 percent of schools with over 1,000 enrollment
- Enroll over 75 percent of the estimated undergraduates in bachelor's degree programs in the United States based on enrollment data from

the U.S. Department of Education's Integrated Postsecondary Education Data System (IPEDS).

Of the approximately 3,396 associate degree–granting schools in the United States, the PayScale College Salary Report 2014–2015 includes 349 schools.

A school's inclusion in or exclusion from the PayScale College Salary Report 2014–2015 is not based on school quality, typical graduate earnings, selectivity, or location within the United States.

PayScale plans to expand the number of schools for future versions of this report as data become available. With more graduate salary data and analysis, we hope eventually to report on nearly all of the bachelor's degree–granting institutions in the United States.

About PayScale: Creator of the largest database of individual compensation profiles in the world containing more than 40 million salary profiles, PayScale, Inc., provides an immediate and precise snapshot of current market salaries to employees and employers through its online tools and software. PayScale's products are powered by innovative algorithms that dynamically acquire, analyze, and aggregate compensation information for millions of individuals in real time. Publisher of the quarterly PayScale Index™, PayScale's subscription software products for employers include PayScale MarketRate™, PayScale Insight™, and PayScale Insight Expert™. PayScale's cloud compensation software is used by more than 3,000 customers including Cummins, Warby Parker, Zendesk, Clemson University, and Covenant Dove. For more information, please visit: www.payscale.com or follow PayScale on Twitter: http://twitter.com/payscale.

Table C.1   Bachelor's Only

School Name	Early Career Median Pay (0–5 YE)	Mid-Career Median Pay (10+ YE)
Harvey Mudd College	$75,600	$133,800
United States Naval Academy (USNA) at Annapolis *	$80,700	$130,000
Massachusetts Institute of Technology (MIT)	$70,300	$128,800
Colgate University	$54,000	$126,600
Stanford University	$62,900	$126,400
California Institute of Technology (Caltech)	$74,800	$126,200
Washington and Lee University	$50,700	$124,300
United States Military Academy (USMA) at West Point *	$75,100	$123,900
Tufts University	$51,900	$123,600
SUNY - Maritime College	$62,100	$121,700
Rice University	$60,000	$119,900
Stevens Institute of Technology	$65,300	$118,700
United States Air Force Academy (USAFA) *	$66,700	$118,400
Harvard University	$57,700	$118,200
Carleton College	$43,700	$117,700
Babson College	$61,300	$117,400
Cooper Union for The Advancement of Science and Art	$61,100	$117,000
Yale University	$58,500	$115,100
Virginia Military Institute (VMI) *	$59,200	$115,000
Haverford College **	$38,600	$115,000
Brown University	$55,100	$114,500
University of California - Berkeley	$59,500	$114,200
Rose-Hulman Institute of Technology (RHIT)	$66,600	$114,100
Princeton University	$60,000	$113,900
University of Pennsylvania	$59,300	$112,200
Carnegie Mellon University (CMU)	$62,300	$111,700
Georgia Institute of Technology	$61,700	$111,700
Santa Clara University	$56,600	$111,700
Cornell University - Ithaca, NY	$58,200	$111,100
Manhattan College	$57,500	$110,800
Clarkson University - Potsdam, NY	$59,900	$110,700
Williams College	$50,200	$110,700
Worcester Polytechnic Institute (WPI)	$62,700	$110,500
NYU Polytechnic School of Engineering	$65,400	$110,400
Rensselaer Polytechnic Institute (RPI)	$62,300	$110,100
Swarthmore College **	$51,000	$109,000

Table C.1 (*Continued*)

School Name	Early Career Median Pay (0–5 YE)	Mid-Career Median Pay (10+ YE)
University of Notre Dame	$55,200	$108,400
Georgetown University - Washington D.C.	$51,000	$108,200
Duke University	$59,500	$108,000
Massachusetts Maritime Academy	$55,200	$107,400
Colorado School of Mines	$67,900	$107,300
Washington University in St. Louis	$55,000	$107,100
Lehigh University	$60,400	$106,300
Dartmouth College	$55,500	$104,700
Vanderbilt University	$56,300	$103,400
New Jersey Institute of Technology (NJIT)	$53,400	$103,200
Kenyon College	$46,400	$102,900
Lafayette College	$57,000	$102,600
University of California - San Diego (UCSD)	$50,600	$102,100
University of Chicago	$48,800	$102,000
Occidental College	$45,600	$101,900
Bucknell University	$56,800	$101,800
University of Rochester	$49,400	$101,700
Villanova University	$53,300	$101,200
Columbia University	$59,200	$101,100
Loyola University - Baltimore, MD	$52,000	$101,000
Union College - Schenectady, NY	$50,800	$101,000
Hofstra University	$46,600	$101,000
Kettering University	$65,100	$100,700
New Mexico Institute of Mining and Technology (New Mexico Tech)	$51,500	$100,500
Gettysburg College	$47,600	$100,400
Boston College	$51,900	$100,200
California Polytechnic State University (CalPoly) - San Luis Obispo	$56,200	$100,100
Drake University	$45,100	$100,000
College of the Holy Cross	$48,500	$99,600
Reed College	$47,500	$99,500
Case Western Reserve University	$58,000	$99,400
University of Virginia (UVA) - Main Campus	$54,100	$99,300
University of California - Irvine (UCI)	$49,300	$99,100
Johns Hopkins University	$58,700	$98,900
Wagner College	$49,800	$98,900
Embry-Riddle Aeronautical University (ERAU) - Prescott, AZ	$53,800	$98,800

(*continued*)

Table C.1 (*Continued*)

School Name	Early Career Median Pay (0–5 YE)	Mid-Career Median Pay (10+ YE)
Northwestern University	$54,200	$98,400
University of the Pacific	$51,500	$98,300
Franklin and Marshall College	$46,300	$98,200
Missouri University of Science and Technology (S&T)	$62,400	$98,100
George Washington University (GWU)	$47,700	$98,100
University of Southern California (USC)	$51,700	$98,000
Whitman College	$41,400	$98,000
Westmont College	$40,300	$98,000
University of California - Davis (UC Davis)	$50,800	$97,900
Texas A&M University - Main Campus	$54,300	$97,700
Lawrence Technological University	$58,300	$97,600
Michigan Technological University	$61,600	$97,300
University of Illinois at Urbana-Champaign (UIUC)	$55,000	$97,100
University of California - Santa Barbara (UCSB)	$47,000	$96,900
University of Massachusetts (UMass) - Lowell Campus	$51,200	$96,600
Bentley University	$58,000	$96,500
Middlebury College **	$51,900	$96,300
University of Texas (UT) - Austin	$52,200	$96,100
Claremont McKenna College **	$50,100	$96,000
University of California - Los Angeles (UCLA)	$50,300	$95,900
Southern Methodist University (SMU)	$50,000	$95,900
New York University (NYU)	$50,000	$95,700
DePauw University	$46,600	$95,700
Rhodes College	$40,600	$95,700
Wentworth Institute of Technology	$55,300	$95,600
Virginia Polytechnic Institute and State University (Virginia Tech)	$53,800	$95,600
Bradley University	$49,900	$95,500
The College of William and Mary	$44,600	$95,500
Loyola Marymount University	$48,900	$95,300
Illinois Institute of Technology (IIT)	$58,300	$95,000
Dickinson College - Carlisle, PA	$44,400	$95,000
South Dakota School of Mines & Technology	$65,600	$94,800
San Jose State University (SJSU)	$51,500	$94,700
Wake Forest University	$53,300	$94,400
Saint Mary's College of California	$50,600	$94,200

Table C.1   (*Continued*)

School Name	Early Career Median Pay (0–5 YE)	Mid-Career Median Pay (10+ YE)
Stony Brook University	$49,800	$94,000
Milwaukee School of Engineering	$60,600	$93,700
West Virginia University Institute of Technology (WVU Tech)	$53,800	$93,500
University of Scranton	$47,900	$93,500
University of Tulsa	$56,800	$93,300
Drexel University	$54,800	$93,200
Colby College	$47,000	$93,200
Marietta College	$43,900	$93,100
Brigham Young University (BYU)	$51,800	$93,000
Oberlin College	$40,200	$92,700
California State Polytechnic University - Pomona	$50,500	$92,500
St. Mary's University - San Antonio, TX	$41,200	$92,500
Macalester College	$41,200	$92,400
Fairfield University	$50,900	$92,100
Pomona College	$46,700	$92,000
University of St. Thomas - St Paul, MN	$46,600	$91,900
Rutgers University - New Brunswick Campus	$51,000	$91,800
Gonzaga University	$47,600	$91,800
University of Washington (UW) - Main Campus	$52,400	$91,700
Auburn University	$47,100	$91,600
University of Maryland - College Park	$52,700	$91,500
Saint Joseph's University (SJU) - Philadelphia, PA	$48,200	$91,500
Bates College **	$44,700	$91,500
Stonehill College	$43,600	$91,500
University of Michigan - Ann Arbor	$56,800	$91,400
St. John's University - Queens, NY	$46,300	$91,400
Wesleyan University - Middletown, CT	$44,400	$91,300
University of San Francisco (USF)	$50,800	$91,200
Brandeis University	$44,600	$91,100
Clemson University	$51,400	$91,000
New York Institute of Technology (NYIT)	$52,500	$90,900
John Carroll University	$48,500	$90,800
Seton Hall University - South Orange, NJ	$46,300	$90,800
Catholic University of America	$45,200	$90,800
CUNY - College of Staten Island	$47,700	$90,700
Willamette University	$41,300	$90,700
Purdue University - Main Campus	$55,400	$90,600
Boston University	$50,100	$90,600
Wofford College - Spartanburg, SC	$44,300	$90,600

(continued)

Table C.1   (*Continued*)

School Name	Early Career Median Pay (0–5 YE)	Mid-Career Median Pay (10+ YE)
Skidmore College	$40,300	$90,400
Rutgers University - Main Campus	$50,800	$90,200
George Mason University	$50,500	$90,200
Marquette University	$49,000	$90,200
Davidson College	$47,200	$90,100
Pratt Institute	$42,900	$89,900
Florida Institute of Technology (Florida Tech)	$56,000	$89,800
Pace University - New York, NY	$51,500	$89,600
University of California - Riverside (UCR)	$45,600	$89,600
Bryant University	$53,700	$89,500
Iona College	$46,800	$89,500
Saint Peters College	$44,000	$89,300
Pacific Lutheran University	$42,100	$89,200
Montana Tech of The University of Montana	$68,400	$88,800
Long Island University - Brooklyn	$51,200	$88,800
Northeastern University	$54,100	$88,600
University of Minnesota - Twin Cities	$49,800	$88,400
California State University - Long Beach (CSULB)	$43,600	$88,400
Hobart William Smith Colleges	$46,900	$88,100
North Carolina State University (NCSU)	$49,600	$88,000
University of Wisconsin (UW) - Madison	$48,500	$88,000
Miami University - Oxford, OH	$49,700	$87,800
CUNY - Bernard M Baruch College	$49,700	$87,700
The Citadel - Military College of South Carolina *	$54,200	$87,600
University of Alabama - Huntsville Campus	$52,000	$87,500
James Madison University (JMU)	$49,400	$87,400
University of Colorado - Boulder (UCB)	$47,900	$87,400
Fashion Institute of Technology - New York, NY	$44,900	$87,300
Hamilton College - Clinton, NY	$57,600	$87,200
Fordham University	$50,200	$87,200
Syracuse University	$48,600	$87,200
Muhlenberg College	$46,900	$87,200
Pennsylvania State University (Penn State) - Main Campus	$51,500	$87,100
SUNY - Binghamton University	$47,200	$87,100
University of Dayton	$50,600	$87,000
Creighton University	$46,500	$87,000
University of Texas - Medical Branch (UTMB)	$58,600	$86,900
University of Richmond	$49,700	$86,800

Table C.1   (*Continued*)

School Name	Early Career Median Pay (0–5 YE)	Mid-Career Median Pay (10+ YE)
Merrimack College	$49,900	$86,700
University of San Diego (USD)	$49,700	$86,700
Ohio Northern University (ONU)	$44,300	$86,700
California Lutheran University (CLU)	$40,900	$86,700
University of Delaware	$49,900	$86,600
Saint John's University (SJU) - Collegeville, MN	$48,900	$86,600
Alfred University	$48,800	$86,600
University of Redlands	$41,300	$86,600
Oregon Institute of Technology (OIT)	$58,500	$86,500
University of Connecticut (UConn) - Main Campus	$51,700	$86,500
Louisiana Tech University	$49,200	$86,500
Elizabethtown College	$40,600	$86,500
Providence College	$50,900	$86,400
CUNY - City College	$52,500	$86,300
Emory University	$51,000	$86,100
La Salle University - Philadelphia, PA	$46,900	$86,100
Washington State University (WSU)	$46,800	$86,000
Butler University	$45,000	$86,000
Monmouth University - West Long Branch, NJ	$43,100	$86,000
Norwich University	$53,200	$85,900
University of Illinois at Chicago	$49,000	$85,900
Tulane University	$45,100	$85,900
Hartwick College	$41,200	$85,800
Touro College - New York, NY	$55,900	$85,700
University of Arizona	$50,000	$85,700
Denison University	$46,500	$85,700
DePaul University	$45,900	$85,600
Rhode Island School of Design (RISD)	$41,800	$85,600
DeVry University - Phoenix, AZ	$49,500	$85,500
University of Houston (UH)	$51,600	$85,400
Lake Forest College	$43,100	$85,400
University of Michigan - Dearborn Campus	$51,800	$85,300
University of Florida (UF)	$48,800	$85,300
Louisiana State University (LSU)	$48,100	$85,300
Prairie View A & M University	$53,800	$85,200
University of Pittsburgh - Main Campus	$47,700	$85,200
New Mexico State University - Main Campus	$46,100	$85,200
University of Hartford	$45,700	$85,200
University of Texas at Dallas	$49,500	$85,000

(*continued*)

Table C.1 (*Continued*)

School Name	Early Career Median Pay (0–5 YE)	Mid-Career Median Pay (10+ YE)
Howard University	$49,300	$85,000
American University - Washington D.C.	$45,100	$85,000
University of Puget Sound	$45,100	$85,000
Walla Walla University	$45,800	$84,900
California State University - Chico	$47,300	$84,800
University of Utah	$47,400	$84,700
University of New Hampshire (UNH) - Main Campus	$45,500	$84,700
University of Massachusetts (UMass) - Amherst Campus	$49,400	$84,600
Iowa State University	$49,300	$84,600
San Diego State University (SDSU) - Main Campus	$45,700	$84,600
University of Maryland, Baltimore County (UMBC)	$50,200	$84,500
University of Portland	$48,800	$84,500
University of Wyoming (UW)	$48,800	$84,400
University of Idaho	$46,700	$84,400
Gannon University	$45,200	$84,300
Dowling College	$47,700	$84,200
Neumann University	$44,700	$84,200
Texas Tech University	$50,500	$84,100
Oregon State University (OSU) - Main Campus	$46,500	$84,100
California State University - Fullerton (CSUF)	$42,600	$84,100
Baylor University	$46,300	$84,000
Clark University - Worcester, MA	$40,700	$84,000
Rochester Institute of Technology (RIT)	$55,900	$83,900
Fairleigh Dickinson University (FDU) - Teaneck, NJ	$48,100	$83,900
Arizona State University (ASU)	$47,700	$83,900
Oklahoma State University (OSU) - Main Campus	$47,100	$83,900
Trinity University	$43,700	$83,900
Widener University - Main Campus	$47,700	$83,800
Saint Anselm College	$48,400	$83,700
San Francisco State University (SFSU)	$47,100	$83,700
Southern Polytechnic State University	$51,000	$83,600
SUNY - Albany	$46,000	$83,500
Colorado College (CC)	$43,900	$83,500
University of Cincinnati (UC)	$47,500	$83,300
Southwestern University	$42,400	$83,300
Samford University	$41,100	$83,300
LeTourneau University	$55,400	$83,100

Table C.1 (*Continued*)

School Name	Early Career Median Pay (0–5 YE)	Mid-Career Median Pay (10+ YE)
Embry-Riddle Aeronautical University (ERAU) - Daytona Beach, FL	$58,500	$83,000
University of Denver	$48,700	$83,000
University of California - Santa Cruz (UCSC)	$46,200	$83,000
University of Massachusetts (UMass) - Dartmouth Campus	$44,600	$83,000
Seattle Pacific University (SPU)	$42,200	$82,900
Michigan State University (MSU)	$47,800	$82,800
The New School	$43,400	$82,800
University at Buffalo (UB)	$47,800	$82,700
Tennessee Technological University (TTU)	$51,100	$82,600
Duquesne University	$44,100	$82,600
Purdue University - Calumet Campus	$43,500	$82,600
Ohio Wesleyan University (OWU)	$41,600	$82,600
Montana State University - Main Campus	$48,900	$82,500
University of Missouri - Columbia	$44,600	$82,500
Rutgers University - Camden Campus	$44,400	$82,500
Le Moyne College	$48,400	$82,400
Barnard College - Columbia University	$46,000	$82,400
University of New England (UNE)	$43,900	$82,400
Molloy College	$59,400	$82,200
University of Oklahoma	$49,700	$82,200
University of Maryland University College (UMUC)	$48,800	$82,200
California State University - Fresno (Fresno State)	$42,200	$82,200
Pacific Union College (PUC)	$50,900	$82,100
University of Iowa (UI)	$44,700	$82,100
Rider University	$44,100	$82,100
Rockhurst University	$50,000	$82,000
Pepperdine University	$47,700	$82,000
University of Phoenix - Tigard, OR	$44,900	$82,000
Art Center College of Design	$57,200	$81,900
Indiana University (IU) - Bloomington	$45,100	$81,900
Thomas More College	$42,600	$81,900
California State University - Sacramento (CSUS)	$46,500	$81,800
University of Texas at El Paso (UTEP)	$45,600	$81,800
Saint Louis University (SLU)	$44,800	$81,800
Siena College	$46,400	$81,700
Thomas Jefferson University	$65,000	$81,600
University of Rhode Island (URI)	$47,100	$81,600
University of Texas at Arlington (UTA)	$51,000	$81,500

(*continued*)

Table C.1   (*Continued*)

School Name	Early Career Median Pay (0–5 YE)	Mid-Career Median Pay (10+ YE)
Holy Family University	$48,100	$81,500
University of Georgia (UGA)	$45,900	$81,500
Xavier University of Louisiana	$41,400	$81,500
Pennsylvania State University (Penn State) - Erie-Behrend College	$50,800	$81,400
Central College	$44,800	$81,400
Wheaton College - Wheaton, IL	$44,800	$81,400
University of Kansas	$43,800	$81,400
Excelsior College	$52,300	$81,300
Texas Christian University (TCU)	$48,400	$81,300
University of Alaska - Fairbanks Campus	$48,500	$81,200
Utah State University - Main Campus	$47,300	$81,200
Mount St. Mary's College - Los Angeles, CA	$48,600	$81,000
Emerson College	$44,300	$81,000
University of Wisconsin (UW) - Platteville Campus	$52,100	$80,900
The College of New Jersey (TCNJ)	$50,300	$80,900
Northern Illinois University (NIU)	$46,500	$80,900
University of Arkansas - Main Campus	$45,400	$80,900
Adelphi University	$47,000	$80,800
Chapman University	$42,200	$80,700
Trinity College	$47,900	$80,600
Montclair State University	$42,600	$80,500
Point Loma Nazarene University	$42,100	$80,500
Knox College	$36,500	$80,500
Thomas Edison State College	$51,400	$80,400
Coleman University	$49,900	$80,400
University of North Carolina at Chapel Hill (UNC)	$46,100	$80,400
Furman University	$44,400	$80,400
Fairleigh Dickinson University (FDU) - Madison, NJ	$49,000	$80,300
Ohio State University (OSU) - Main Campus	$48,000	$80,300
University of Vermont (UVM)	$44,800	$80,300
University of Mary Washington	$44,100	$80,200
Lamar University	$50,500	$80,100
William Jewell College	$44,600	$80,100
Western Michigan University (WMU)	$43,400	$80,100
West Chester University	$42,200	$80,100
California College of the Arts	$43,900	$80,000
Bloomfield College	$37,800	$80,000
DeVry University - Pomona, CA	$49,200	$79,900

Table C.1   (*Continued*)

School Name	Early Career Median Pay (0–5 YE)	Mid-Career Median Pay (10+ YE)
California State University - East Bay (CSUEB)	$46,000	$79,900
St. Olaf College	$41,700	$79,900
SUNY - Institute of Technology (SUNYIT)	$50,100	$79,800
University of Nebraska - Lincoln	$43,400	$79,800
The University of Texas (UT) - Health Science Center at San Antonio	$53,900	$79,700
Oakland University - Rochester Hills, MI	$45,400	$79,700
California State University - San Bernardino (CSUSB)	$43,300	$79,700
University of New Haven	$46,800	$79,600
CUNY - Hunter College	$43,800	$79,600
Southern University and A&M College	$42,000	$79,600
Oregon Health and Science University (OHSU)	$66,800	$79,500
Kansas State University (KSU)	$48,000	$79,500
Whittier College **	$40,200	$79,500
DeVry University - Columbus, OH	$47,100	$79,400
Mississippi State University (MSU)	$46,800	$79,400
University of Nevada - Reno (UNR)	$45,700	$79,400
Idaho State University (ISU)	$45,200	$79,400
California State University - Northridge (CSUN)	$43,700	$79,400
Washington & Jefferson College	$39,600	$79,400
Nichols College	$38,500	$79,300
Wilkes University	$47,900	$79,200
Colorado State University (CSU)	$46,000	$79,200
Wayne State University - Detroit, MI	$43,700	$79,200
University of Louisiana (UL) at Lafayette	$43,700	$79,200
Ursinus College	$40,700	$79,200
Grove City College	$47,200	$79,000
University of Tennessee	$44,900	$79,000
Concordia University - Irvine, CA	$41,500	$79,000
Gustavus Adolphus College	$40,800	$79,000
Drew University	$45,300	$78,800
Western Washington University	$45,100	$78,800
Western New England College	$52,900	$78,700
Rowan University	$43,500	$78,700
West Virginia University (WVU) - Main Campus	$46,300	$78,600
Illinois Wesleyan University (IWU)	$42,800	$78,600
DeVry University - Federal Way, WA	$46,100	$78,500
Temple University	$44,700	$78,500

(*continued*)

Table C.1 (*Continued*)

School Name	Early Career Median Pay (0–5 YE)	Mid-Career Median Pay (10+ YE)
Grinnell College	$43,100	$78,500
Southwestern Oklahoma State University	$41,100	$78,500
DeVry University - North Brunswick, NJ	$47,900	$78,400
Academy of Art University	$47,900	$78,200
Suffolk University	$44,000	$78,200
Bloomsburg University of Pennsylvania	$42,900	$78,200
University of Louisiana - Monroe Campus	$41,600	$78,200
Illinois State University	$43,800	$78,100
Nova Southeastern University	$47,500	$78,000
Loyola University - Chicago, IL	$43,800	$78,000
SUNY - Geneseo	$40,300	$78,000
Seattle University	$46,100	$77,900
Bellarmine University	$40,900	$77,900
CUNY - Brooklyn College	$43,400	$77,800
The Richard Stockton College of New Jersey	$39,300	$77,800
Wellesley College	$45,900	$77,700
University of Pittsburgh - Johnstown Campus	$44,800	$77,700
Westminster College - Salt Lake City, UT	$49,800	$77,600
Taylor University - Upland, IN	$39,800	$77,600
University of Colorado - Denver Campus	$46,100	$77,500
Central Washington University (CWU)	$45,000	$77,300
California State University - Los Angeles (CSULA)	$43,600	$77,300
Eckerd College	$40,100	$77,300
Pennsylvania State University (Penn State) - Harrisburg Campus	$52,300	$77,200
Valparaiso University	$48,800	$77,200
Robert Morris University (RMU) - Moon Township, PA	$44,300	$77,200
University of New Mexico (UNM)	$43,100	$77,200
Saint Francis University	$41,400	$77,200
Quinnipiac University	$50,800	$77,000
Ohio University - Main Campus	$43,600	$77,000
Lewis & Clark College	$38,700	$77,000
Farmingdale State College	$44,100	$76,900
University of Wisconsin (UWEC) - Eau Claire	$43,500	$76,900
Smith College	$41,300	$76,900
St. Thomas Aquinas College	$36,500	$76,900
Loma Linda University	$65,100	$76,800
Ferris State University	$46,500	$76,800

Table C.1   (*Continued*)

School Name	Early Career Median Pay (0–5 YE)	Mid-Career Median Pay (10+ YE)
Wittenberg University	$45,900	$76,800
University of Findlay	$44,200	$76,800
Towson University	$44,300	$76,700
University of Missouri - Kansas City (UMKC)	$44,200	$76,700
SUNY - Purchase College	$41,600	$76,700
University of Alaska - Anchorage Campus	$52,100	$76,600
South Dakota State University (SDSU)	$45,800	$76,600
St. Lawrence University	$44,700	$76,600
University of Nebraska at Omaha	$44,200	$76,600
University of Alabama - Main Campus	$43,600	$76,600
Florida State University (FSU)	$42,700	$76,600
Ramapo College of New Jersey	$40,800	$76,600
Hiram College	$37,500	$76,500
University of Maine at Orono	$45,100	$76,400
Dominican College - Orangeburg, NY	$42,500	$76,400
Old Dominion University	$42,200	$76,400
North Central College - Naperville, IL	$41,400	$76,400
New England Institute of Technology	$49,000	$76,300
Ithaca College	$44,000	$76,300
Sonoma State University	$46,400	$76,200
Marymount University - Arlington, VA	$45,600	$76,100
National University	$45,100	$76,100
Northeastern Illinois University	$42,700	$76,100
Simmons College	$48,600	$76,000
University of Miami (UM) - Florida	$47,800	$76,000
Stevenson University	$40,700	$76,000
North Carolina A&T State University	$48,300	$75,900
University of Toledo	$45,500	$75,800
Biola University	$39,300	$75,800
Cleveland State University	$45,800	$75,600
University of Minnesota - Duluth Campus	$43,800	$75,600
Cabrini College	$43,200	$75,600
Sacred Heart University - Fairfield, CT	$48,500	$75,500
Carroll College - Helena, MT	$47,200	$75,500
Post University	$46,000	$75,500
Birmingham Southern College	$41,100	$75,500
University of Massachusetts (UMass) - Boston Campus	$48,700	$75,400
North Dakota State University (NDSU)	$48,100	$75,400

(*continued*)

Table C.1   (*Continued*)

School Name	Early Career Median Pay (0–5 YE)	Mid-Career Median Pay (10+ YE)
Southwestern College - Winfield, KS	$45,200	$75,400
Roger Williams University	$45,100	$75,400
California State University - Bakersfield (CSUB)	$44,100	$75,400
Western Connecticut State University	$43,300	$75,400
Utah Valley University	$44,500	$75,300
Hawaii Pacific University	$42,800	$75,300
Texas Tech University - Health Sciences Center	$57,600	$75,200
University of Colorado at Colorado Springs	$46,000	$75,200
Houston Baptist University	$42,700	$75,200
Christian Brothers University	$42,000	$75,200
Humboldt State University	$41,000	$75,200
Messiah College	$45,400	$75,100
Marist College	$43,400	$75,100
Western State College of Colorado	$42,800	$75,100
East Stroudsburg University (ESU)	$40,500	$75,100
University of South Carolina - Main Campus	$43,100	$75,000
Central Connecticut State University	$42,800	$75,000
Sarah Lawrence College **	$39,000	$75,000
University of North Dakota	$47,500	$74,900
University of Oregon	$42,900	$74,900
Nebraska Wesleyan University (NWU)	$36,700	$74,900
Saint Cloud State University	$44,700	$74,800
Olivet Nazarene University	$39,600	$74,700
Regis University - Denver, CO	$51,100	$74,600
Carroll University - Waukesha, WI	$37,200	$74,600
Calvin College	$42,700	$74,500
Whitworth University	$40,800	$74,500
Monmouth College - Monmouth, IL	$38,000	$74,500
Tuskegee University	$50,700	$74,400
Western Illinois University	$42,000	$74,400
York College - York, PA	$43,300	$74,300
Hamline University	$41,300	$74,300
Virginia Commonwealth University (VCU)	$42,900	$74,100
CUNY - Queens College	$42,300	$74,100
Beloit College	$39,200	$74,100
Augustana College - Sioux Falls, SD	$38,800	$74,100
University of Bridgeport (UB)	$43,900	$74,000
Dallas Baptist University	$41,400	$74,000
Indiana University-Purdue University - Fort Wayne (IPFW)	$40,900	$74,000

Table C.1   (*Continued*)

School Name	Early Career Median Pay (0–5 YE)	Mid-Career Median Pay (10+ YE)
Weber State University	$49,800	$73,900
Pennsylvania College of Technology	$48,700	$73,900
DeVry University - Kansas City, MO	$46,700	$73,900
DeVry University - Chicago, IL	$47,900	$73,800
University of Evansville	$46,800	$73,800
Long Island University - C W Post Campus	$45,400	$73,800
University of Central Florida (UCF)	$42,600	$73,800
University of North Texas (UNT)	$41,400	$73,800
Embry-Riddle Aeronautical University (ERAU) Worldwide	$55,700	$73,700
College for Creative Studies	$42,500	$73,700
University of North Carolina at Charlotte (UNCC)	$43,500	$73,600
University of South Florida - Main Campus	$43,100	$73,600
California State University - Stanislaus	$43,000	$73,600
Otterbein College	$41,000	$73,600
Bridgewater State College	$39,100	$73,600
University of Wisconsin (UWM) - Milwaukee	$43,800	$73,500
Florida International University (FIU)	$43,000	$73,500
Concordia University - Austin, TX	$41,700	$73,500
Cedarville University	$43,500	$73,400
Benedictine University	$43,600	$73,300
Assumption College - Worcester, MA	$46,300	$73,200
Worcester State University	$43,000	$73,200
William Paterson University	$41,500	$73,200
Franklin University	$41,400	$73,200
University of St. Francis	$41,000	$73,200
Troy University	$39,500	$73,200
Eastern New Mexico University - Main Campus	$38,400	$73,200
Clarion University of Pennsylvania	$36,400	$73,200
University of Baltimore	$48,700	$73,100
New Jersey City University	$46,000	$73,100
Metropolitan State University	$45,600	$73,100
Metropolitan State College of Denver (MSCD)	$41,600	$73,100
Allegheny College - Meadville, PA	$36,200	$73,100
DeVry University - Irving, TX	$47,600	$73,000
Southern Illinois University (SIU) - Carbondale Campus	$45,600	$73,000
Eastern Connecticut State University	$41,000	$73,000
Columbus State University	$35,200	$73,000
Georgia State University	$44,200	$72,900

(*continued*)

Table C.1   (*Continued*)

School Name	Early Career Median Pay (0–5 YE)	Mid-Career Median Pay (10+ YE)
Bowling Green State University - Bowling Green, OH	$41,600	$72,900
Texas A&M University - Corpus Christi Campus	$45,000	$72,800
Texas State University - San Marcos Campus	$43,700	$72,800
St. Ambrose University	$40,600	$72,800
University of Mount Union	$40,600	$72,800
Hampton University	$40,200	$72,800
D'Youville College	$49,600	$72,700
Lewis University	$47,000	$72,700
Salisbury University	$46,300	$72,700
University of Memphis (U of M)	$43,600	$72,700
University of Hawaii at Manoa	$43,600	$72,700
University of Indianapolis	$42,200	$72,700
St. John Fisher College - Rochester, NY	$41,700	$72,700
Framingham State University	$41,900	$72,600
Misericordia University	$40,300	$72,600
Cornell College - Mount Vernon, IA	$37,500	$72,600
University of Houston Downtown (UHD)	$47,000	$72,500
University of Kentucky (UK)	$45,800	$72,500
University of Akron - Main Campus	$45,500	$72,500
Truman State University	$39,900	$72,500
Minnesota State University - Mankato Campus	$46,500	$72,400
West Texas A & M University	$44,100	$72,400
Millersville University of Pennsylvania	$40,600	$72,400
University of Phoenix - Colorado Springs, CO	$50,400	$72,300
Arcadia University	$35,700	$72,300
Sam Houston State University	$42,400	$72,200
Roosevelt University	$41,800	$72,200
Kean University	$40,100	$72,200
Geneva College	$39,700	$72,200
University of La Verne	$39,500	$72,200
Loyola University - New Orleans, LA	$39,400	$72,200
Wright State University - Main Campus	$45,400	$72,100
University of Nevada - Las Vegas (UNLV)	$43,900	$72,100
Elon University	$43,500	$72,100
University of Mississippi	$41,000	$72,100
Notre Dame of Maryland University	$51,000	$72,000
Indiana University-Purdue University - Indianapolis (IUPUI)	$43,600	$72,000

Table C.1   (*Continued*)

School Name	Early Career Median Pay (0–5 YE)	Mid-Career Median Pay (10+ YE)
SUNY - College at Oneonta	$42,200	$72,000
University of Alabama - Birmingham Campus	$41,200	$72,000
Youngstown State University (YSU)	$39,400	$71,900
Xavier University	$47,100	$71,800
University of Wisconsin (UW) - La Crosse Campus	$42,400	$71,800
Canisius College	$38,300	$71,800
Western Governors University (WGU)	$49,500	$71,700
University of Wisconsin (UW) - Stout Campus	$45,900	$71,700
Eastern Washington University	$44,000	$71,700
Cameron University - Lawton, OK	$41,000	$71,700
Strayer University - Washington D.C.	$50,100	$71,600
Northwest Missouri State University	$39,800	$71,600
Morehouse College	$50,300	$71,500
University of South Alabama	$47,000	$71,400
School of Visual Arts (SVA) - New York, NY	$45,400	$71,400
Elmhurst College	$43,800	$71,400
California State University - San Marcos (CSUSM)	$43,600	$71,400
Alma College	$39,400	$71,400
Linfield College	$45,400	$71,300
National Louis University	$44,300	$71,300
University of North Florida (UNF)	$43,200	$71,300
Hope College	$44,800	$71,200
Augsburg College	$49,600	$71,100
Northern Arizona University (NAU)	$42,800	$71,100
South Carolina State University	$42,700	$71,100
Indiana University of Pennsylvania (IUP)	$40,000	$71,100
College of Mount St. Joseph	$37,700	$71,100
Notre Dame de Namur University (NDNU)	$48,400	$71,000
Florida Agricultural and Mechanical (A&M) University (FAMU)	$43,600	$71,000
Bob Jones University	$41,300	$71,000
Eastern Illinois University	$39,300	$71,000
Georgia Southern University	$42,700	$70,900
Southern Illinois University (SIU) - Edwardsville Campus	$44,800	$70,800
University of Wisconsin (UWW) - Whitewater	$41,700	$70,800
Azusa Pacific University	$43,300	$70,700
California State University - Dominguez Hills (CSUDH)	$42,200	$70,700

(*continued*)

Table C.1   (*Continued*)

School Name	Early Career Median Pay (0–5 YE)	Mid-Career Median Pay (10+ YE)
Saginaw Valley State University (SVSU)	$39,400	$70,700
Coe College	$46,700	$70,600
University of Louisville	$43,200	$70,600
Texas Southern University	$40,300	$70,600
Walden University	$40,100	$70,600
Colorado Christian University	$42,900	$70,500
Park University	$42,600	$70,500
Augusta State University	$36,800	$70,500
University of Detroit Mercy (UDM)	$46,000	$70,400
Portland State University (PSU)	$43,700	$70,400
The College of Wooster	$38,800	$70,400
Texas A&M University - Kingsville Campus	$54,300	$70,300
Mount Holyoke College	$41,300	$70,300
CUNY - John Jay College Criminal Justice	$39,300	$70,300
Murray State University	$36,900	$70,300
DeVry University - Decatur, GA	$44,600	$70,200
Mercer University	$47,100	$70,100
Pacific University	$44,000	$70,100
College of Our Lady of the Elms	$45,400	$70,000
Northwood University - Midland, MI	$43,900	$70,000
Eastern Michigan University	$41,600	$70,000
Rhode Island College	$40,300	$70,000
St. Joseph's College (SJC) - Brooklyn, NY	$35,000	$70,000
University of Missouri - St. Louis Campus	$42,400	$69,900
University of Tennessee at Chattanooga (UTC)	$41,100	$69,900
Stephen F. Austin State University (SFA)	$40,900	$69,900
Augustana College - Rock Island, IL	$40,600	$69,900
Bryn Mawr College **	$44,600	$69,800
Lipscomb University	$40,200	$69,800
McKendree University	$39,900	$69,800
Slippery Rock University	$39,500	$69,800
High Point University	$42,700	$69,700
Massachusetts College of Art and Design	$41,300	$69,700
University of Montana	$38,600	$69,700
University of Mary Hardin-Baylor (UMHB)	$48,600	$69,600
SUNY - College at Plattsburgh	$37,500	$69,600
Columbia Southern University	$50,000	$69,500
Colorado Technical University - Colorado Springs Campus	$45,900	$69,500

Table C.1   (*Continued*)

School Name	Early Career Median Pay (0–5 YE)	Mid-Career Median Pay (10+ YE)
Abilene Christian University	$45,500	$69,500
Midwestern State University (MSU)	$42,000	$69,500
Texas Woman's University	$44,000	$69,400
Southern Oregon University	$40,500	$69,400
Winthrop University	$39,600	$69,400
Colorado State University (CSU) - Pueblo Campus	$44,300	$69,300
Kennesaw State University	$40,900	$69,300
Lee University - Cleveland, TN	$34,000	$69,300
Salem State University	$39,600	$69,200
Southwest Minnesota State University (SMSU)	$37,300	$69,100
Medical College of Georgia	$53,100	$69,000
Connecticut College	$47,000	$69,000
Susquehanna University	$43,600	$69,000
Harding University	$39,600	$69,000
Fitchburg State College	$42,000	$68,900
Franklin Pierce University	$46,000	$68,800
University of New Orleans (UNO)	$44,300	$68,800
University of Phoenix - Jersey City, NJ	$44,100	$68,800
University of South Dakota	$42,600	$68,800
Wichita State University	$42,300	$68,800
University of Wisconsin (UW) - River Falls Campus	$38,400	$68,800
DeSales University	$45,200	$68,700
Andrews University	$44,800	$68,700
North Park University	$44,400	$68,700
Mississippi College	$38,800	$68,700
Lynchburg College	$38,100	$68,700
Florida Atlantic University (FAU)	$44,400	$68,600
University of Southern Mississippi (USM)	$39,600	$68,600
Georgia Southwestern State University	$39,400	$68,600
Saint Mary's College - Notre Dame, IN	$44,400	$68,500
University of Texas at San Antonio (UTSA)	$42,700	$68,500
Johnson & Wales University (JWU) - Providence, RI	$40,400	$68,500
Oklahoma Christian University	$37,800	$68,500
SUNY - College at Oswego	$36,700	$68,500
McNeese State University	$46,400	$68,400
Angelo State University	$44,700	$68,400
Berkeley College - New York, NY	$42,200	$68,400
Southern Utah University	$41,200	$68,400
ITT Technical Institute - Indianapolis, IN	$49,800	$68,300

(*continued*)

Table C.1   *(Continued)*

School Name	Early Career Median Pay (0–5 YE)	Mid-Career Median Pay (10+ YE)
Boise State University (BSU)	$44,700	$68,300
SUNY - Empire State College	$44,000	$68,300
Salve Regina University	$47,600	$68,200
Manchester College - North Manchester, IN	$39,900	$68,200
Jacksonville State University (JSU)	$38,500	$68,200
Webster University	$38,400	$68,200
Capella University	$46,400	$68,100
Christopher Newport University	$44,300	$68,100
University of Phoenix - Phoenix, AZ	$44,200	$68,100
Eastern Kentucky University	$39,800	$68,100
University of Central Missouri	$39,700	$68,100
Carson Newman College	$41,700	$68,000
Lake Superior State University - Sault Ste Marie, MI	$40,900	$68,000
Point Park University	$38,400	$68,000
Texas Wesleyan University	$37,700	$68,000
Georgian Court University	$35,000	$68,000
Alvernia University	$44,500	$67,800
Philadelphia University	$43,900	$67,800
Central Michigan University	$41,400	$67,700
Indiana State University	$41,300	$67,700
Ball State University (BSU)	$39,500	$67,700
Buena Vista University	$34,700	$67,700
CUNY - Lehman College	$40,700	$67,600
Grand Canyon University	$49,600	$67,500
Barry University	$42,300	$67,500
Texas Lutheran University **	$38,600	$67,500
Wayland Baptist University	$37,500	$67,500
Mount Saint Mary College - Newburgh, NY	$44,600	$67,400
Campbell University	$43,600	$67,400
Armstrong Atlantic State University (AASU)	$41,100	$67,400
Plymouth State University	$40,400	$67,400
Mount Mary College - Milwaukee, WI	$39,400	$67,400
Nicholls State University	$38,900	$67,400
Niagara University	$38,600	$67,400
Capital University	$45,500	$67,300
Delaware Valley College	$43,900	$67,300
Union University - Jackson, TN	$44,800	$67,200
University of Tampa	$41,800	$67,200

Table C.1   (*Continued*)

School Name	Early Career Median Pay (0–5 YE)	Mid-Career Median Pay (10+ YE)
Rivier College	$41,800	$67,200
Houghton College	$31,700	$67,200
Viterbo University	$45,900	$67,100
University of the Arts (UArts) - Philadelphia, PA	$39,900	$67,100
SUNY - New Paltz	$39,200	$67,100
University of West Florida (UWF)	$38,700	$67,100
Marian University - Fond Du Lac, WI	$38,300	$67,000
Pittsburg State University	$37,900	$67,000
University of North Alabama (UNA)	$36,900	$67,000
St. Xavier University	$42,900	$66,900
East Tennessee State University (ETSU)	$43,100	$66,800
Oklahoma Baptist University (OBU)	$38,500	$66,800
Hardin-Simmons University (HSU)	$46,600	$66,700
North Carolina Wesleyan College (NCWC)	$45,500	$66,700
University of Northern Colorado	$39,800	$66,700
Northern State University	$37,300	$66,700
Washburn University	$41,300	$66,600
Texas A&M University - Commerce Campus	$35,500	$66,600
University of Southern Maine (USM)	$43,200	$66,500
Mercy College	$41,900	$66,500
Kent State University (KSU)	$39,500	$66,500
Athens State University	$37,700	$66,500
Morningside College	$32,900	$66,500
Jacksonville University	$46,300	$66,400
University of Northern Iowa	$41,700	$66,400
Bellevue University - Bellevue, NE	$43,800	$66,300
Savannah College of Art and Design (SCAD)	$40,300	$66,300
Keene State College	$39,600	$66,300
Austin Peay State University	$39,200	$66,300
Carthage College	$40,700	$66,200
Governors State University	$37,800	$66,200
King College - Bristol, TN	$35,900	$66,200
Immaculata University	$43,500	$66,100
Rollins College	$43,100	$66,100
University of Wisconsin (UW) - Stevens Point Campus	$39,200	$66,100
Kutztown University of Pennsylvania	$38,900	$66,100
Gwynedd-Mercy College	$44,900	$66,000
Woodbury University	$44,000	$66,000

(*continued*)

Table C.1 (*Continued*)

School Name	Early Career Median Pay (0–5 YE)	Mid-Career Median Pay (10+ YE)
Charleston Southern University (CSU)	$40,600	$66,000
Arkansas State University (ASU)	$40,300	$66,000
Walsh College of Accountancy and Business Administration	$46,300	$65,900
Saint Mary's University of Minnesota	$44,600	$65,900
Northern Kentucky University (NKU)	$43,800	$65,800
Aurora University	$40,100	$65,800
College of Charleston	$39,100	$65,800
Albertus Magnus College	$43,800	$65,700
University of Southern Indiana	$41,300	$65,700
Marshall University	$37,200	$65,600
College of the Ozarks	$32,200	$65,600
Winona State University	$41,500	$65,500
Millikin University	$41,100	$65,500
Florida Southern College	$39,200	$65,500
Roberts Wesleyan College	$43,600	$65,400
University of Wisconsin (UWP) - Parkside	$38,400	$65,400
Cleary University	$41,600	$65,300
Missouri State University (MSU)	$38,800	$65,300
Saint Leo University	$38,400	$65,300
University of Texas - Pan American (UTPA)	$43,200	$65,200
Marymount Manhattan College	$43,200	$65,200
Eastern University	$43,000	$65,200
Minnesota State University - Moorhead Campus	$39,100	$65,200
Indiana University (IU) - New Albany	$38,400	$65,200
Shepherd University	$42,700	$65,100
Moravian College and Moravian Theological Seminary	$45,200	$65,000
Radford University	$42,500	$64,900
Central State University	$35,200	$64,900
Utica College	$42,900	$64,800
Concordia University - Mequon, WI	$40,700	$64,800
Our Lady of the Lake University (OLLU)	$40,700	$64,800
Siena Heights University	$39,800	$64,800
Frostburg State University	$39,800	$64,700
Albright College	$44,800	$64,600
University of Phoenix - Reno, NV	$38,500	$64,600
Keuka College	$44,800	$64,500
Baldwin-Wallace College	$41,200	$64,500
University of Central Oklahoma (UCO)	$39,000	$64,500

Table C.1   (*Continued*)

School Name	Early Career Median Pay (0–5 YE)	Mid-Career Median Pay (10+ YE)
Valdosta State University (VSU)	$37,200	$64,500
Cedar Crest College	$46,200	$64,400
Southern Connecticut State University (SCSU)	$43,200	$64,400
Emporia State University	$35,200	$64,400
Oral Roberts University (ORU)	$41,300	$64,300
Longwood University	$39,800	$64,300
Southern New Hampshire University	$42,300	$64,200
John Brown University	$41,000	$64,200
University of Central Arkansas	$38,700	$64,200
East Carolina University (ECU)	$41,200	$64,000
Middle Tennessee State University (MTSU)	$41,000	$64,000
Columbus College of Art And Design	$37,500	$64,000
Virginia State University (VSU)	$37,300	$64,000
Cardinal Stritch University	$45,300	$63,900
Maryville University of Saint Louis	$44,700	$63,900
Anderson University - Anderson, IN	$39,100	$63,900
Baker University	$45,200	$63,800
Simpson College - Indianola, IA	$38,400	$63,800
University of Wisconsin (UW) - Oshkosh Campus	$42,900	$63,700
SUNY - College at Potsdam	$36,500	$63,700
Langston University	$41,000	$63,600
Berklee College of Music	$41,000	$63,600
Arkansas Tech University	$38,500	$63,600
ITT Technical Institute - Tallahassee, FL	$37,600	$63,400
North Carolina Central University	$34,700	$63,400
Shippensburg University of Pennsylvania	$41,100	$63,300
Western Kentucky University	$40,300	$63,300
Carlow University	$32,400	$63,300
Georgia College & State University (GCSU)	$41,200	$63,200
Luther College	$45,700	$63,100
Madonna University	$43,200	$63,100
Columbia College - Chicago, IL	$37,900	$63,100
University of Nebraska at Kearney	$35,500	$63,100
University of Texas at Tyler	$48,000	$63,000
Southeast Missouri State University	$38,200	$62,900
Marian University - Indianapolis, IN	$44,800	$62,800
Husson University	$37,000	$62,800
Tennessee State University	$47,900	$62,700
George Fox University	$43,700	$62,700

(*continued*)

Table C.1   (*Continued*)

School Name	Early Career Median Pay (0–5 YE)	Mid-Career Median Pay (10+ YE)
Western Carolina University	$41,200	$62,700
SUNY - College at Brockport	$38,000	$62,700
Alabama A&M University (AAMU)	$44,400	$62,600
Oklahoma City University	$40,400	$62,500
University of Phoenix - Temple Terrace, FL	$38,500	$62,500
Alabama State University (ASU)	$36,500	$62,500
Midamerica Nazarene University	$42,000	$62,400
California University of Pennsylvania (Cal U)	$40,400	$62,400
Appalachian State University	$40,000	$62,300
West Liberty University	$36,500	$62,300
Mansfield University of Pennsylvania	$35,400	$62,300
Concordia College - Moorhead, MN	$41,700	$62,200
University of West Georgia	$40,000	$62,200
St. Catherine University - St. Paul, MN	$42,400	$62,100
Concordia University - Saint Paul, MN	$40,000	$62,100
Nyack College	$37,400	$62,100
Wilmington College - Wilmington, OH	$40,700	$62,000
Huntingdon College	$40,300	$61,700
Coastal Carolina University	$38,900	$61,700
University of North Carolina at Greensboro (UNCG)	$38,500	$61,700
Stetson University	$36,400	$61,700
Henderson State University	$36,000	$61,700
Fort Lewis College	$40,700	$61,600
University of Illinois at Springfield	$37,600	$61,600
Missouri Western State University	$36,100	$61,600
Ursuline College	$50,000	$61,500
Trident University International	$47,400	$61,500
Delaware State University	$39,500	$61,500
Fort Hays State University (FHSU)	$39,000	$61,500
Centenary College	$33,000	$61,500
Upper Iowa University	$39,300	$61,400
Trevecca Nazarene University	$45,500	$61,300
Morehead State University (Kentucky)	$33,000	$61,300
Baker College - Flint, MI	$40,800	$61,200
Columbia College - Columbia, MO	$39,500	$61,200
Lock Haven University	$35,400	$61,200
West Virginia State University	$31,300	$61,200
Bemidji State University (BSU)	$39,900	$61,100
Davenport University	$39,300	$61,100
Evergreen State College	$39,300	$61,100

Table C.1   (*Continued*)

School Name	Early Career Median Pay (0–5 YE)	Mid-Career Median Pay (10+ YE)
Belmont University	$39,000	$61,000
Bridgewater College	$38,000	$61,000
Southern Nazarene University	$41,000	$60,900
Indiana Institute Of Technology	$46,900	$60,800
Bethel University - Saint Paul, MN	$45,200	$60,800
Westfield State University	$42,500	$60,800
University of North Carolina at Wilmington (UNCW)	$41,300	$60,800
Limestone College	$40,900	$60,800
Northwestern State University	$40,200	$60,800
Edinboro University of Pennsylvania	$35,100	$60,800
Ohio Dominican University	$42,100	$60,700
Liberty University	$38,200	$60,700
Clarke College - Dubuque, IA	$37,100	$60,700
Lander University	$35,500	$60,700
Mercyhurst College	$40,400	$60,600
William Penn University	$41,700	$60,500
Indiana Wesleyan University (IWU)	$41,400	$60,500
SUNY - College at Cortland	$38,100	$60,500
Auburn University - Montgomery	$41,100	$60,300
North Georgia College and State University	$40,900	$60,300
University of South Carolina - Upstate Campus	$39,200	$60,300
Ashland University	$35,600	$60,300
Wheeling Jesuit University	$35,400	$60,200
Medaille College	$41,600	$60,100
Robert Morris University (RMU) - Chicago, IL	$40,300	$59,900
Malone University	$40,300	$59,900
Montana State University - Billings Campus	$38,400	$59,800
Winston-Salem State University	$43,300	$59,700
American Public University System	$42,000	$59,600
Grand View University (GVU)	$41,200	$59,600
University of Phoenix - Grand Rapids, MI	$40,500	$59,600
Lindenwood University	$37,800	$59,600
Berry College	$36,800	$59,600
University of North Carolina at Asheville (UNCA)	$35,300	$59,600
University of Mary	$44,800	$59,500
Clark Atlanta University (CAU)	$40,400	$59,500
Avila University	$44,600	$59,400
SUNY - Fredonia	$36,800	$59,400
Grand Valley State University	$40,600	$59,300

(*continued*)

Table C.1 (*Continued*)

School Name	Early Career Median Pay (0–5 YE)	Mid-Career Median Pay (10+ YE)
Southeastern Oklahoma State University	$45,200	$59,200
Grambling State University	$41,100	$59,200
Ripon College	$39,400	$59,200
Brenau University	$41,600	$59,100
Lakeland College - Plymouth, WI	$44,100	$59,000
School of the Art Institute of Chicago	$39,200	$59,000
Delta State University	$37,800	$59,000
Transylvania University	$34,300	$59,000
University of Phoenix - Columbia, SC	$35,600	$58,900
Northeastern State University	$40,000	$58,700
Alverno College	$40,300	$58,600
Bluffton University	$36,500	$58,600
Belmont Abbey College	$42,400	$58,500
Minot State University	$45,300	$58,400
Tarleton State University (TSU)	$42,600	$58,300
Morgan State University	$41,500	$58,300
Wingate University	$30,600	$58,300
Gardner-Webb University	$38,700	$58,200
University of Wisconsin (UW) - Green Bay Campus	$34,400	$58,200
Mountain State University	$47,200	$58,000
Bowie State University (BSU)	$41,300	$58,000
Southeastern University	$36,300	$58,000
Southeastern Louisiana University	$40,700	$57,900
Wilmington University	$40,400	$57,900
Evangel University	$35,900	$57,900
University of Arkansas - Pine Bluff Campus	$35,000	$57,900
Mount Mercy University	$41,700	$57,800
SUNY - College at Buffalo	$39,800	$57,600
Francis Marion University	$31,500	$57,600
The University of Tennessee at Martin (UT Martin)	$38,400	$57,500
University of Michigan - Flint Campus	$40,800	$57,400
American InterContinental University (AIU) - Online	$39,800	$57,400
Meredith College	$36,500	$57,400
Northern Michigan University	$44,100	$57,300
Marywood University	$41,700	$57,200
Jackson State University (JSU)	$39,900	$57,200
Spring Arbor University	$32,100	$57,100
Clayton State University	$41,000	$57,000
University of Phoenix - Savannah, GA	$33,300	$56,500

Table C.1   (*Continued*)

School Name	Early Career Median Pay (0–5 YE)	Mid-Career Median Pay (10+ YE)
Missouri Southern State University (MSSU)	$36,300	$56,300
Tusculum College	$33,400	$56,300
University of Arkansas - Little Rock Campus	$39,900	$56,200
Thiel College	$38,200	$56,000
Heidelberg University	$36,500	$55,900
Belhaven University	$39,600	$55,700
Waynesburg University	$44,900	$55,500
Wartburg College	$43,800	$55,400
Mount Vernon Nazarene University (MVNU)	$34,200	$55,400
Coppin State University (CSU)	$44,200	$55,300
Sullivan University	$40,300	$55,300
Western Oregon University	$38,400	$55,300
Friends University	$44,300	$55,200
University of The Incarnate Word	$42,400	$55,100
Massachusetts College of Liberal Arts (MCLA)	$34,800	$55,100
Chicago State University (CSU)	$38,900	$55,000
Drury University	$36,900	$55,000
University of Phoenix - Saint Louis Park, MN	$38,900	$54,900
Briar Cliff University	$35,400	$54,900
Nazareth College of Rochester	$36,800	$54,600
Mount Olive College	$35,500	$54,600
Culinary Institute of America (CIA) - Hyde Park, NY	$34,300	$54,500
North Central University	$36,700	$54,400
Maryland Institute College of Art	$37,100	$54,000
Colorado Technical University - Online	$44,000	$53,900
Lesley University	$40,800	$53,700
Norfolk State University	$40,400	$52,800
Wayne State College - Wayne, NE	$35,500	$52,500
Fayetteville State University	$33,700	$52,500
University of Northwestern - St. Paul	$38,400	$52,400
Averett University	$38,200	$52,300
DeVry University - Miramar, FL	$38,600	$52,100
University of Maine at Augusta (UMA)	$33,000	$51,800
Concord University	$32,200	$51,800
William Woods University	$35,900	$51,600
Guilford College	$42,000	$51,300
Savannah State University (SSU)	$36,200	$51,300
Fairmont State University	$39,200	$51,200
Fontbonne University	$38,900	$51,200

(*continued*)

Table C.1 (*Continued*)

School Name	Early Career Median Pay (0–5 YE)	Mid-Career Median Pay (10+ YE)
University of North Carolina at Pembroke (UNCP)	$41,800	$50,600
Southwest Baptist University	$34,900	$50,600
Bethel College - Mishawaka, IN	$34,100	$50,600
Miami Dade College (MDC)	$45,200	$50,100
Indiana University (IU) - South Bend	$37,300	$49,500
Ashford University	$37,000	$49,500
Mississippi University for Women	$40,300	$49,300
University of Maine at Farmington (UMF)	$45,200	$49,100
University of Phoenix - Chattanooga, TN	$43,300	$49,000
Faulkner University	$38,200	$48,300
College of New Rochelle	$36,700	$48,300
Bethel University - McKenzie, TN	$37,300	$47,400
Coker College	$32,700	$46,800
University of Montevallo	$32,500	$46,700
University of Phoenix - Raleigh, NC	$37,000	$46,500
Chestnut Hill College	$35,900	$43,500
Shaw University	$34,600	$40,300

*Data represents those in the civilian labor force, not active service members.
**Results for these schools based on last year's report due to insufficient data in 2014. These schools are not included on the All Graduates ranking since that is a new feature this year.

Table C.2   Associate Only

School Name	Early Career Median Pay (0–5 YE)	Mid-Career Median Pay (10+ YE)
Fashion Institute of Technology - New York, NY	$42,300	$71,000
San Diego City College	$42,200	$70,900
De Anza College	$46,200	$70,000
Lee College	$39,900	$69,000
NHTI-Concord's Community College	$40,200	$68,700
CUNY - Queensborough Community College	$36,600	$68,500
Mercer County Community College (MCCC)	$40,100	$67,300
Bakersfield College	$46,300	$67,200
Los Angeles Trade Technical College	$34,600	$66,300
Dunwoody College of Technology	$42,400	$66,100
Orange County Community College - Middletown, NY	$37,800	$65,300
Citrus College	$29,500	$65,300
Texas State Technical College (TSTC) - Waco Campus	$42,300	$65,000
Heald College - Concord, CA	$41,000	$64,600
Ranken Technical College	$42,000	$64,300
Renton Technical College	$43,100	$64,000
Excelsior College	$56,200	$63,800
Prince George's Community College	$44,300	$63,800
Orange Coast College - Costa Mesa, CA	$39,000	$63,800
Bellevue College	$39,300	$63,600
Oakton Community College	$48,100	$63,200
San Jacinto College	$40,800	$63,200
Middlesex Community College - Bedford, MA	$43,900	$63,000
County College of Morris	$38,400	$62,700
ITT Technical Institute - DeSoto, TX	$38,300	$62,700
Massachusetts Bay Community College	$42,400	$62,600
CUNY - Kingsborough Community College	$36,400	$62,600
Collin College - McKinney, TX	$38,000	$62,500
Santa Rosa Junior College	$37,300	$62,500
The Community College of Baltimore County	$46,700	$62,300
Utah Valley University	$33,800	$62,200
Pearl River Community College	$37,200	$62,000
Universal Technical Institute of Arizona Inc	$35,700	$62,000
Briarcliffe College	$39,500	$61,900
ITT Technical Institute - San Diego, CA	$43,000	$61,800
Weber State University	$39,800	$61,700
Santa Ana College	$37,600	$61,700

(continued)

Table C.2 (*Continued*)

School Name	Early Career Median Pay (0–5 YE)	Mid-Career Median Pay (10+ YE)
Corning Community College	$32,200	$61,600
SUNY - Westchester Community College	$36,400	$61,500
CUNY - Borough of Manhattan Community College	$32,100	$61,500
Harper College	$41,600	$61,400
El Camino College	$39,100	$61,400
Union County College	$42,600	$61,200
Lincoln Technical Institute - East Windsor, CT	$36,300	$61,200
Pennsylvania State University (Penn State) - Main Campus	$42,600	$61,100
Pueblo Community College	$40,300	$61,100
Grossmont College	$42,600	$60,900
City College of San Francisco	$42,300	$60,900
Community College of Rhode Island	$40,600	$60,700
San Diego Mesa College	$38,800	$60,700
Nassau Community College (NCC)	$33,500	$60,700
San Jose City College	$35,700	$60,300
Navarro College	$41,700	$60,100
Anne Arundel Community College	$38,200	$60,000
Saddleback Community College	$30,800	$60,000
Northern Virginia Community College	$44,900	$59,900
Minnesota State Community & Technical College	$41,900	$59,900
Burlington County College - Pemberton, NJ	$41,600	$59,700
Phoenix College	$40,200	$59,400
Massasoit Community College	$43,200	$59,300
Bergen Community College	$37,900	$59,300
Tacoma Community College	$42,900	$59,200
Triton College	$39,400	$59,200
Quincy College	$48,800	$59,100
Pensacola State College	$43,900	$59,100
Palm Beach State College	$35,300	$59,100
ITT Technical Institute - West Houston, TX	$47,900	$59,000
Arapahoe Community College	$39,500	$59,000
Culinary Institute of America (CIA) - Hyde Park, NY	$35,300	$59,000
Miami Dade College (MDC)	$34,800	$58,900
Brookdale Community College	$38,200	$58,800
Lorain County Community College	$41,400	$58,700
ITT Technical Institute - Phoenix, AZ	$38,400	$58,700

Table C.2   (*Continued*)

School Name	Early Career Median Pay (0–5 YE)	Mid-Career Median Pay (10+ YE)
Essex County College	$32,700	$58,700
New England Institute of Technology	$42,300	$58,500
Waubonsee Community College	$40,200	$58,500
Caldwell Community College and Technical Institute	$34,200	$58,500
Salt Lake Community College (SLCC)	$40,600	$58,400
Rock Valley College	$37,600	$58,400
Allegany College of Maryland	$43,200	$58,300
Manchester Community College - Manchester, CT	$39,800	$58,300
University of Cincinnati (UC)	$38,800	$58,200
Cerritos College	$36,800	$58,200
Dakota County Technical College	$36,800	$58,000
Mott Community College	$33,500	$58,000
Indian Hills Community College	$41,400	$57,900
Santa Barbara City College	$40,700	$57,800
Northcentral Technical College (NTC)	$40,400	$57,800
Polk State College	$38,500	$57,800
Tarrant County College	$36,100	$57,800
MiraCosta College	$34,900	$57,800
Minneapolis Community & Technical College	$35,400	$57,700
Central Texas College	$35,900	$57,600
Oklahoma City Community College	$35,100	$57,600
Montgomery County Community College - Central Campus	$39,400	$57,400
Berkeley College - New York, NY	$38,400	$57,400
Fresno City College	$34,800	$57,400
Highline Community College	$34,700	$57,400
Tompkins Cortland Community College	$39,000	$57,300
Brown College	$36,100	$57,300
Cypress College	$35,100	$57,200
North Shore Community College	$39,200	$57,100
Waukesha County Technical College (WCTC)	$35,900	$57,100
Technical Career Institutes (TCI)	$42,500	$57,000
Greenville Technical College - Greenville, SC	$39,200	$57,000
Shoreline Community College	$39,500	$56,900
Illinois Central College	$37,300	$56,900
Mt. San Antonio College	$36,800	$56,900
Boise State University (BSU)	$42,700	$56,800
Houston Community College System (HCCS)	$37,300	$56,800

(*continued*)

Table C.2 (*Continued*)

School Name	Early Career Median Pay (0–5 YE)	Mid-Career Median Pay (10+ YE)
Mesa Community College (MCC)	$36,100	$56,800
Gulf Coast Community College	$39,600	$56,600
Richland College - Dallas, TX	$34,300	$56,600
Springfield Technical Community College (STCC)	$45,400	$56,500
Hudson Valley Community College (HVCC)	$36,500	$56,500
Amarillo College	$44,900	$56,400
Nashville State Community College	$31,500	$56,300
Northern Essex Community College	$41,300	$56,200
Austin Community College District	$39,700	$56,100
Midland College	$43,800	$56,000
Southeast Technical Institute	$34,800	$56,000
WyoTech - Laramie, WY	$34,600	$56,000
Lone Star College System	$40,600	$55,900
Kent State University (KSU)	$46,500	$55,800
Elgin Community College	$41,300	$55,800
Heald College - Salida, CA	$33,800	$55,800
Cincinnati State Technical and Community College	$40,500	$55,600
Northampton County Area Community College	$36,400	$55,600
Riverside Community College	$35,700	$55,600
Palomar College	$36,200	$55,500
The Art Institute of Seattle	$40,600	$55,400
Brevard Community College - Cocoa, FL	$35,600	$55,400
San Antonio College	$40,900	$55,300
Midlands Technical College (MTC)	$33,200	$55,300
Southeast Community College Area	$38,500	$55,200
American River College	$40,500	$55,100
Owens Community College	$35,900	$55,100
York Technical College - Rock Hill, SC	$34,400	$55,100
Del Mar College	$49,000	$55,000
Suffolk County Community College	$40,300	$55,000
Spokane Community College (SCC)	$38,500	$55,000
Front Range Community College (FRCC)	$35,100	$55,000
Lakeland Community College - Kirtland, OH	$34,800	$55,000
Southwest Tennessee Community College	$32,800	$55,000
CUNY - LaGuardia Community College	$41,000	$54,900
East Los Angeles College	$37,400	$54,900
ITT Technical Institute - Indianapolis, IN	$38,100	$54,800
Idaho State University (ISU)	$37,100	$54,800

Table C.2   (*Continued*)

School Name	Early Career Median Pay (0–5 YE)	Mid-Career Median Pay (10+ YE)
Hillsborough Community College	$36,900	$54,700
Fayetteville Technical Community College	$30,200	$54,700
SUNY - College of Technology at Canton	$47,400	$54,600
Pikes Peak Community College (PPCC)	$29,200	$54,600
St Paul College - St Paul, MN	$39,400	$54,500
Fashion Institute of Design & Merchandising	$37,200	$54,500
Chaffey College	$31,800	$54,500
James A Rhodes State College	$43,000	$54,300
Gwinnett Technical College - Lawrenceville, GA	$42,200	$54,300
Normandale Community College	$41,400	$54,300
Quinsigamond Community College	$38,200	$54,300
Broward Community College	$36,100	$54,300
Santa Monica College	$51,400	$54,200
Pasco-Hernando Community College	$42,800	$54,200
College of DuPage	$40,300	$54,200
DeVry University - Chicago, IL	$38,200	$54,200
Tyler Junior College	$34,600	$54,200
Delaware County Community College	$33,300	$54,200
St. Cloud Technical and Community College	$34,600	$54,000
Kalamazoo Valley Community College (KVCC)	$34,200	$54,000
St Petersburg College	$34,200	$54,000
Delaware Technical and Community College - Stanton-Wilmington Campus	$47,200	$53,900
Clark College - Vancouver, WA	$35,100	$53,900
Edison State College - Fort Myers, FL	$33,600	$53,900
Inver Hills Community College	$39,300	$53,800
Johnson County Community College	$37,900	$53,800
Henry Ford Community College	$44,400	$53,700
San Joaquin Delta College	$39,400	$53,600
Green River Community College	$42,200	$53,500
Grayson County College (GCC)	$40,500	$53,500
SUNY - College of Technology at Alfred	$35,900	$53,500
Casper College	$48,400	$53,300
Jefferson Community College	$33,700	$53,300
Full Sail University	$33,600	$53,300
Ivy Tech Community College - Indianapolis, IN	$32,300	$53,300
Schoolcraft College	$39,100	$53,200
Chattanooga State Community College	$38,500	$53,200
Macomb Community College	$38,500	$53,200

(*continued*)

Table C.2   (*Continued*)

School Name	Early Career Median Pay (0–5 YE)	Mid-Career Median Pay (10+ YE)
Indian River State College	$36,000	$53,200
Montgomery College - Rockville, MD	$35,600	$53,200
Luzerne County Community College	$30,900	$53,200
Pittsburgh Technical Institute (PTI)	$37,000	$53,100
University of Akron - Main Campus	$36,500	$53,100
Fullerton College	$36,000	$53,100
Kansas City Kansas Community College	$43,100	$53,000
Moraine Valley Community College	$42,500	$53,000
Zane State College	$41,100	$53,000
Anoka Technical College	$40,600	$53,000
Mt Hood Community College	$38,200	$53,000
Sinclair Community College	$37,600	$53,000
Iowa Western Community College	$31,200	$53,000
Columbia College - Columbia, MO	$29,600	$52,900
Kellogg Community College (KCC)	$34,700	$52,800
Erie Community College	$34,600	$52,800
North Dakota State College of Science (NDSCS)	$35,900	$52,700
Trident Technical College	$33,200	$52,700
Anoka-Ramsey Community College	$41,800	$52,600
Central Piedmont Community College	$35,800	$52,600
Columbus State Community College	$32,000	$52,600
Western Iowa Tech Community College	$30,800	$52,500
Florence Darlington Technical College	$36,700	$52,400
Hocking College	$32,000	$52,400
Yakima Valley Community College	$40,000	$52,200
Wake Technical Community College	$35,600	$52,200
Dutchess Community College	$35,400	$52,200
Edmonds Community College	$39,100	$52,100
Lake Washington Technical College	$44,300	$52,000
Mississippi Gulf Coast Community College	$34,700	$52,000
Tulsa Community College	$38,000	$51,900
Art Institute of Fort Lauderdale	$36,400	$51,800
Columbia State Community College (CSCC)	$39,200	$51,800
Vincennes University	$38,700	$51,800
Strayer University - Washington D.C.	$43,700	$51,800
Seminole State College of Florida - Sanford	$32,300	$51,800
Hinds Community College	$31,700	$51,800
ITT Technical Institute - Akron, OH	$37,400	$51,700
St. Philip's College	$40,200	$51,700

Table C.2 (*Continued*)

School Name	Early Career Median Pay (0–5 YE)	Mid-Career Median Pay (10+ YE)
Ferris State University	$39,200	$51,700
Harcum College	$48,800	$51,700
Moraine Park Technical College	$34,900	$51,700
Gadsden State Community College	$33,200	$51,700
Rose State College	$38,500	$51,600
Berkeley College - Woodland Park, NJ	$39,500	$51,500
Stark State College of Technology	$37,200	$51,500
Mid-State Technical College	$30,600	$51,500
Century Community and Technical College	$41,600	$51,400
South University - The Art Institute of Dallas	$34,300	$51,400
North Central State College	$32,800	$51,400
Walters State Community College	$42,100	$51,200
Community College of Allegheny County	$40,700	$51,200
Red Rocks Community College	$39,900	$51,200
Madison Area Technical College	$36,500	$51,200
Oakland Community College - Bloomfield Hills, MI	$36,200	$51,200
College of Central Florida	$34,800	$51,200
Onondaga Community College	$33,900	$51,100
Western Kentucky University	$27,100	$51,000
Naugatuck Valley Community College	$42,400	$50,900
Fox Valley Technical College (FVTC)	$37,900	$50,900
Milwaukee Area Technical College (MATC)	$39,900	$50,800
Florida State College at Jacksonville	$38,100	$50,800
Niagara County Community College	$35,200	$50,800
Northeast Wisconsin Technical College	$31,600	$50,800
Washtenaw Community College (WCC)	$39,600	$50,600
Chippewa Valley Technical College (CVTC)	$36,900	$50,600
Forsyth Technical Community College	$37,400	$50,500
Lansing Community College	$36,300	$50,500
Grand Rapids Community College (GRCC)	$34,700	$50,500
Hennepin Technical College	$37,200	$50,400
Jackson State Community College (JSCC)	$36,700	$50,400
Portland Community College (PCC)	$35,900	$50,400
Des Moines Area Community College	$34,600	$50,400
ITT Technical Institute - Tallahassee, FL	$32,800	$50,400
Finger Lakes Community College	$32,500	$50,300
Bristol Community College	$41,600	$50,200
Wallace Community College	$36,800	$50,200
Horry-Georgetown Technical College	$35,900	$50,200

(*continued*)

Table C.2 (*Continued*)

School Name	Early Career Median Pay (0–5 YE)	Mid-Career Median Pay (10+ YE)
Gateway Technical College - Kenosha, WI	$35,700	$50,200
Clark State Community College - Springfield, OH	$40,500	$50,100
Pima Community College	$35,500	$50,100
Lane Community College - Eugene, OR	$34,000	$50,100
Delgado Community College	$35,500	$50,000
Lehigh Carbon Community College	$40,300	$49,900
Harrisburg Area Community College	$38,800	$49,900
Camden County College	$30,200	$49,900
Jefferson State Community College	$36,000	$49,800
Valencia Community College	$33,500	$49,700
City Colleges of Chicago - Wilbur Wright College	$34,400	$49,600
Cuyahoga Community College	$37,600	$49,400
Baker College - Muskegon, MI	$34,800	$49,400
Kirkwood Community College	$34,100	$49,300
J. Sargeant Reynolds Community College	$38,400	$49,200
Everett Community College	$41,300	$49,100
Guilford Technical Community College (GTCC)	$36,400	$49,100
John Tyler Community College	$43,200	$49,000
College of Southern Nevada	$40,700	$49,000
Santa Fe College - Gainesville, FL	$32,900	$49,000
Pennsylvania College of Technology	$38,800	$48,900
Parkland College	$37,000	$48,900
State College of Florida-Manatee-Sarasota (SCF)	$32,800	$48,900
CUNY - Bronx Community College	$32,400	$48,900
The Art Institute of Pittsburgh	$31,100	$48,900
Hesser College	$30,700	$48,900
College of Lake County	$46,200	$48,800
Westmoreland County Community College	$35,400	$48,700
Western Technical College - La Crosse, WI	$36,500	$48,600
John C Calhoun State Community College	$35,900	$48,500
Davidson County Community College	$36,200	$48,400
Sullivan University	$31,000	$48,400
Chemeketa Community College	$34,100	$48,300
Tri-County Technical College	$39,800	$48,200
Georgia Perimeter College	$37,400	$48,200
North Seattle Community College	$36,200	$48,000
South Central College	$39,500	$47,900

Table C.2   (*Continued*)

School Name	Early Career Median Pay (0–5 YE)	Mid-Career Median Pay (10+ YE)
Joliet Junior College	$33,300	$47,900
Southwestern Illinois College	$33,000	$47,900
Blackhawk Technical College	$43,400	$47,800
Northeast Community College	$32,700	$47,800
Robert Morris University (RMU) - Chicago, IL	$32,100	$47,800
Wayne Community College (WCC)	$36,900	$47,600
Roane State Community College	$36,500	$47,600
SUNY - College of Technology at Delhi	$33,500	$47,500
Southern Maine Community College	$38,100	$47,300
Danville Area Community College (DACC)	$40,000	$47,200
Spartanburg Community College	$39,400	$47,200
Community College of Philadelphia	$34,200	$47,200
Cape Fear Community College	$34,200	$47,100
Central New Mexico Community College	$35,000	$47,000
Mount Wachusett Community College	$39,700	$46,900
Wisconsin Indianhead Technical College (WITC)	$35,200	$46,900
Monroe Community College (MCC)	$31,000	$46,800
Kilgore College	$41,400	$46,700
Delta College - University Center, MI	$36,100	$46,700
Holyoke Community College	$38,100	$46,500
Keiser University - Ft. Lauderdale, FL	$37,300	$46,300
Baker College - Flint, MI	$33,200	$46,200
Alexandria Technical College	$37,700	$46,100
Sierra College	$35,800	$45,700
Central Community College	$31,100	$45,400
Wallace State Community College - Hanceville Campus	$37,900	$45,000
Wayne County Community College District	$39,400	$44,700
Butler Community College - El Dorado, KS	$37,600	$44,700
Daytona State College	$37,100	$44,700
Kaplan University - Davenport, IA	$32,300	$44,600
Gaston College	$31,900	$44,500
Darton College	$45,900	$44,400
University of Phoenix - Phoenix, AZ	$32,000	$44,400
Fisher College	$37,800	$44,100
Pitt Community College	$39,200	$43,900
Dekalb Technical College	$37,500	$43,700
Spokane Falls Community College	$29,900	$43,700
Tidewater Community College	$33,700	$43,300

(*continued*)

Table C.2   (*Continued*)

School Name	Early Career Median Pay (0–5 YE)	Mid-Career Median Pay (10+ YE)
American InterContinental University (AIU) - Online	$31,700	$43,300
Alamance Community College (ACC)	$33,100	$43,100
Bryant and Stratton College - Buffalo, NY	$30,100	$43,100
Genesee Community College	$34,800	$42,300
University of Phoenix - Online Campus	$36,000	$40,700
Lakeshore Technical College (LTC)	$37,400	$40,000
Colorado Technical University - Online	$31,300	$40,000
Davenport University	$31,800	$39,800
Ashford University	$33,000	$39,500
National College of Business & Technology	$27,600	$36,800

Notes

Chapter 1

1. Danica Patrick. CNN Interview. November 2012. http://www.cnn.com/video/?
   /video/bestoftv/2012/11/28/exp-early-best-advice-patrick.cnn&iref=allsearch
   &video_referrer=http%3A%2F%2Fwww.cnn.com%2Fsearch%2F%3Fquery
   %3Ddanica%2Bpatrick%2Bearly%2Bstart%26x%3D-1010%26y%3D-31%
   26primaryType%3Dmixed
2. Chinese proverb, often quoted by Warren Buffett. http://www.brainyquote.com
   /quotes/quotes/w/warrenbuff409214.html
3. Fidelity Investments, Fidelity Viewpoints. January 2014. "Five habits of 401(k)
   millionaires." https://www.fidelity.com/viewpoints/retirement/how-to-become-
   a-millionaire-with-a-401k
4. National Association of Colleges and Employers, Job Outlook 2014 Spring
   Update.
5. Bureau of Labor Statistics, June 2014 Employment Report.
6. David Leonhardt, "The Reality of Student Debt Is Different from the Clichés,"
   New York Times, June 24, 2014.
7. Mark Kantrowitz, senior vice president and publisher of Edvisors and author of
   Filing the FAFSA.
8. National Association of Colleges and Employers (NACE), *Salary Survey,* April
   2014, www.naceweb.org/salary-resources/salary-survey.aspx.
9. Jennifer Cheeseman Day and Eric C. Newburger, "The Big Payoff: Educational
   Attainment and Synthetic Estimates of Work-Life Earnings," U.S. Census
   Bureau, July 2002, http://www.census.gov/prod/2002pubs/p23-210.pdf.
10. "Think You Know the Next Gen Investor? Think Again," UBS Investor Watch
    1Q 2014.
11. "Young America and Its Vices: Beer. McDonald's. Starbucks.," App, Level
    Money, July 2014.

12. National Credit Union Administration, 2013 Annual Report, http://www.ncua .gov/Legal/Documents/Reports/AR2013.pdf.

13. Bankrate.com, Financial Security Index, February 2014.

14. National Foundation for Credit Counseling (NFCC), "NFCC Offers Five Steps to Finding $1,000 for Holiday Spending," Press Release, July 21, 2014.

Chapter 2

1. Bureau of Labor Statistics, 1985 through April 2014. http://data.bls.gov/pdq /SurveyOutputServlet

2. David Leonhardt, "The Reality of Student Debt Is Different from the Clichés," *New York Times,* June 24, 2014.

3. "Making Student Loans More Affordable," White House Factsheet, June 9, 2014.

4. "How America Saves for College," Sallie Mae and Ipsos, April 10, 2014.

5. "Yes, a College Degree Is Still Worth It," CNNMoney, http://money.cnn.com /2014/06/24/news/economy/college-worth-it/index.html.

6. Bureau of Labor Statistics, June 2014, Employment Situation Summary, www.bls.gov

7. "Wells Fargo Millennial Study," 2014. Wells Fargo Wealtgh, Brokerage and Retirement. https://www08.wellsfargomedia.com/downloads/pdf/press/2q14pr -millennials-save-survey.pdf

8. "How America Saves for College," Sallie Mae and Ipsos, April 10, 2014.

9. Anthony P. Carnevale and Ban Cheah, "Hard Times, College Majors, Unemployment and Earnings 2013: Not All College Degrees are Created Equal." Center on Education and the Workforce. Georgetown University.

10. "Attainment of College and Career Readiness," ACT, August 2014.

11. Carnevale and Cheah, "Hard Times."

12. "College Degrees with the Best and Worst Value," Bankrate.com, June 2013.

Chapter 3

1. "Young Adults, Student Debt and Economic Well-Being," Pew Research. May 14, 2014. http://www.pewsocialtrends.org/2014/05/14/young-adults-student-debt -and-economic-well-being/

2. "Retirees' Social Security Checks Garnished for Student Loans," U.S. Treasury Analysis for *CNNMoney,* August 24, 2014.

3. Richard Fry and Andrea Caumont, "5 Key Findings About Student Debt," Pew Research, May 14, 2014, http://www.pewresearch.org/fact-tank/2014/05/14/5 -key-findings-about-student-debt/.

4. Fidelity Investments, "How to Pay Off Debt," *Fidelity Viewpoints,* April 3, 2014.

5. Ibid.

6. "Top 10 Student Loan Tips for Recent Graduates," Project on Student Debt, http://projectonstudentdebt.org/recent_grads.vp.html.

Chapter 4

1. Job Openings and Labor Turnover Survey (JOLTS), U.S. Department of Labor, August 2014.

2. U.S. Bureau of Labor Statistics; *CNNMoney*.

3. Employment Situation Summary, U.S. Bureau of Labor Statistics, http://www.bls.gov/news.release/empsit.nr0.htm.

4. Labor Force Statistics from the Current Population Survey, U.S. Bureau of Labor Statistics, August 2014.

5. Sam Ro, "Apple Has More Money Than All These Different Countries," *Business Insider,* April 7, 2014.

6. "10 Fastest Growing States," *CNNMoney,* http://money.cnn.com/gallery/news/economy/2014/06/11/fastest-growing-state-economies/index.html?iid=SF_E_Lead.

7. "Growing Labor Shortage on the Horizon in Mature Economies," The Conference Board, September 2, 2014.

8. Jaison R. Abel, "College May Not Pay Off for Everyone," *New York Fed,* September 4, 2014.

9. Ibid.

Chapter 5

1. Sean Bisceglia, "Outside Opinion: Millennials Frustrate HR Execs," *Chicago Tribune,* http://www.chicagotribune.com/business/ct-hiring-millennials-outside-opinion-0907-biz-20140905-story.html.

2. Charles Riley, "Facebook Is 69% Male and Mostly White," *CNNMoney,* June 26, 2014.

3. "New Aon Hewitt Survey Shows 2014 Variable Pay Spending Spikes to Record High Level," Aon Hewitt, Mediaroom, August 2014.

4. Matt Egan, "Talent Wars: Silicon Valley vs. Wall Street," *CNNMoney,* August 22, 2014.

5. Edelman Berland, "Freelancing in America: A National Study of the New Work-force."September 4, 2014. https://www.freelancersunion.org/blog/dispatches/2014/09/04/53million/

6. CareerBuilder. "Fifty-eight Percent of Employers Have Caught a Lie on a Resume, According to a New CareerBuilder Survey." August 7, 2014.

http://www.careerbuilder.com/share/aboutus/pressreleasesdetail.aspx?sd=8%2F7%2F2014&id=pr837&ed=12%2F31%2F2014

7. "America Employed 2014," Express Employment Professionals. July 23, 2014 http://www.expresspros.com/subsites/americaemployed/Qualities-Employers-Look-for-in-Candidates.aspx

8. Sheryl Sandberg, *Lean In* (New York: Knopf, 2013). www.leanin.org/book "In her own words."

9. "Women CEOS of the Fortune 1000," Catalyst.org, November 2014, http://www.catalyst.org/knowledge/women-ceos-fortune-1000.

10. "The Gender Wage Gap by Occupation 2013," Institute for Women's Policy Research, Fact Sheet, April 2014.

11. Sheryl Sandberg, *Lean In*. (New York: Knopf, 2013). www.leanin.org/book "In her own words."

12. Christine Romans and Ali Velshi, *How to Speak Money: The Language and Knowledge You Need Now* (Hoboken, NJ: Wiley, 2012).

13. Belinda Luscombe, "Women's Salaries: At Last, Women on Top," *Time,* September 1, 2010, http://content.time.com/time/business/article/0,8599,2015274,00.html.

14. Belinda Luscombe, "Confidence Woman: Facebook's Sheryl Sandberg is on a mission to change the balance of power. Why she just might pull it off."

Chapter 6

1. Richard Fry and Jeffrey Passel, "In Post-Recession Era, Young Adults Drive Continuing Rise in Multi-Generational Living," Pew Research, July 17, 2014.

2. Standard & Poor's (S&P)/Case-Shiller Home Price Indices, data through June 2014.

3. Ibid.

4. Peter Morici, "Where to Invest Your Money in an Aging Bull Market,"University of Maryland, March 10, 2014.

5. National Association of Realtors, April 2014.

6. Heather Long, "Housing Market Is a 'Crapshoot,'" *CNNMoney,* July 7, 2014.

7. Sam Khater, "Generation Renter. Millennials Delaying Milestone Life Events, Such as Homeownership, to Pursue Different Goals," CoreLogic, June 2014.

8. Ben Brody, "Millennial-Driven Housing Boom Coming," *CNNMoney,* June 27, 2014, http://money.cnn.com/2014/06/26/real_estate/harvard-millennials-housing/index.html.

9. Ibid.

10. "Housing Market Gridlock Caused by Underwater Gen Xers," Zillow, Q2 Negative Equity Report. August 2014.

11. National Association of Realtors. Q2 2014, "Median Sales Price of Existing Single-Family Homes for Metropolitan Areas," http://www.realtor.org/sites /default/files/reports/2014/embargoes/2014-q2-metro-home-prices/metro-home-prices-q2-2014-single-family-2014-08-12.pdf

12. "Best Cities for Millennial Homeowners," *CNNMoney*, National Association of Realtors, August 4, 2014.

13. "Rent More Expensive in 88% of Major Markets," Zillow, August 21, 2014.

14. U.S. Census Bureau 2012 American Community Survey.

15. Christine Romans, *Smart Is the New Rich: If You Can't Afford It—Put It Down* (Hoboken, NJ: Wiley, 2010).

Chapter 7

1. "Two-Thirds of Engaged Couples Express Negative Attitudes Toward Discussing Money. NFCC Advises Couple Stalk Before They Walk," National Foundation for Credit Counseling (NFCC), July 2013, http://money.cnn.com/2013/06/13/news /money-marriage/index.html?iid=EL, http://www.nfcc.org/NewsRoom /newsreleases/DiscussingMoney.cfm.

2. Ibid.

3. Tami Luhby, "Millennials Say No to Marriage," *CNNMoney*, July 14, 2014, http://money.cnn.com/2014/07/20/news/economy/millennials-marriage/.

4. Bankrate.com.

5. Jeffrey Dew, "Bank on It. Thrifty Couples Are Happiest," National Marriage Project, 2009, http://www.stateofourunions.org/2009/bank_on_it.php.

6. Blake Ellis, "Big Student Loans? Consider Life Insurance," *CNNMoney*, August 5, 2014, http://money.cnn.com/2014/08/05/pf/college/student-loans-insurance /index.html.

7. Blake Ellis, "Grieving Parents Drowning in $200,000 Student Loan Debt Receive Relief," *CNNMoney*, July 30, 2014, http://money.cnn.com/2014/07/30/pf /parents-student-loans/index.html.

8. 2014 Wells Fargo Millennial Study, June 2014, http://money.cnn.com/2014/06 /11/pf/millennials-debt/index.html.

Chapter 8

1. "36% of Americans Have Not Saved Any Money for Retirement," Bankrate.com, August 18, 2014.

2. Standard & Poor's (S&P) Dow Jones Indexes, January 1926–June 2014.

3. "How to Turn $200 a Month into $5 Million," Motley Fool, August 17, 2014.

4. "U.S. Stock Ownership Stays at a Record Low," Gallup Poll, May 8, 2013.

5. "36% of Americans Have Not Saved Any Money for Retirement," Bankrate.com, August 18, 2014.

6. "Think You Know the Next Gen Investor? Think Again," UBS Investor Watch, Q1 2014.

7. Melanie Hickens, "No 401(k)? You've Got Options," *CNNMoney,* April 1, 2014.

8. King Digital Entertainment, U.S. Securities and Exchange Commission (SEC) Filing, http://www.sec.gov/Archives/edgar/data/1580732 /000119312514056089/d564433df1.htm#toc564433_2.

9. GrubHub Inc., U.S. Securities and Exchange Commission (SEC) Filing, http://www.sec.gov/Archives/edgar/data/1594109/000119312514075544 /d647121ds1.htm#toc647121_3.

10. Google stock chart August 19, 2004 to August 19, 2014, https://www.google .com/finance?q=NASDAQ%3AGOOG

Chapter 9

1. "More Millennials Say No to Credit Cards," Bankrate.com, September 2014, http://money.cnn.com/2014/09/08/pf/millennials-credit-cards/index.html?iid =HP_LN.

2. Ibid.

3. Claes Bell, "Overdraft Protection. Do You Need It?" Bankrate.com, http://www.bankrate.com/finance/savings/bank-overdraft-protection-do-you -need-it-1.aspx.

4. Credit Card Repayment Calculator, Board of Governors of the Federal Reserve System, Federal Reserve.

5. "Rand Paul Takes on Fed, Lunch in Epic Twitter Rant," CNBC, December 23, 2013, http://www.cnbc.com/id/101293594#.

6. Peter Valdes-Dapena, "Youngest Car Shoppers Are Buying More Cars," J.D. Power and Associates, *CNNMoney,* August 4, 2014.

About the Author

Christine Romans is CNN's Chief Business Correspondent and anchor of *Early Start with John Berman and Christine Romans* weekday mornings on CNN. Romans has covered some of the most important stories of our time: the tech bubble and bust; the terrorist attack on September 11, 2001; the stock market crash of 2008; two hurricanes; four presidential elections; and every conceivable market move in between.

She has hosted CNN hourly specials on everything from Bernie Madoff, in *Madoff: Secrets of a Scandal* to the decline of the U.S. auto industry, in *How the Wheels Came Off*, the state of the American Dream, and *In God We Trust*, an examination of faith and money in the wake of the financial crisis.

Smart Is the New Rich: Money Guide for Millennials is her third book. In 2010 she published *Smart Is the New Rich: If You Can't Afford It—Put It Down*, and two years later she coauthored *How to Speak Money: The Language and Knowledge You Need to Know Now* with Ali Velshi.

Romans won an Emmy award for her work on the series *Exporting America,* about globalization and outsourcing U.S. manufacturing and high-tech jobs overseas. She has been honored for her work by Mothers Against Drunk Driving (MADD), the National Foundation for Women Legislators, and the Alliance for Women in the Media, and twice by her alma mater, Iowa State University.

A proud Iowa native, she graduated from ISU with a degree in journalism and French. She learned the business and economic beat as a reporter in the rough-and-tumble commodities pits in Chicago, where she eventually covered a wide variety of subjects including agriculture, currencies, stocks, bonds,

Federal Reserve policy, and derivatives, first for Knight-Ridder Financial News and then for Reuters. In 1999, she moved to CNN*fn*, CNN's financial news channel, first as a reporter from the floor of the New York Stock Exchange and later as an anchor of CNN*fn*'s flagship programs *Street Sweep* and *Money Gang*. She lives in New Jersey with her husband and three young sons.

Index